Bead Tube Jewelry

Peyote & brick stitch designs for 30+ necklaces, bracelets, and earrings

Nancy Zellers

KALMBACH BOOKS

Kalmbach Books
21027 Crossroads Circle
Waukesha, Wisconsin 53186
www.Kalmbach.com/Books

Published in 2011
15 14 13 12 11   2 3 4 5 6

Manufactured in the United States of America

ISBN: 978-0-87116-417-9

Publisher's Cataloging-in-Publication Data

Zellers, Nancy.
  Bead tube jewelry : peyote & brick stitch designs for 30+ necklaces, bracelets,
  and earrings / Nancy Zellers.

  p. : ill. (chiefly col.) ; cm.

  ISBN: 978-0-87116-417-9

  1. Beadwork–Patterns. 2. Beadwork–Handbooks, manuals, etc. 3. Jewelry
  making–Handbooks, manuals, etc. I. Title.

TT860 .Z45 2010
745.5942

Contents

Introduction

Things I Like

I like little beads. I like sewing one little bead to another little bead, over and over and over again. I like writing instructions for how to sew one little bead to another little bead. I like teaching other people how to sew one little bead to another little bead. I like taking little beads and turning them into something different, bigger. This book is about taking a very simple, slightly larger thing—a bead tube—and seeing how many wearable things you can create. Simple things, complex things, sweet things, elegant things, playful things, plain things, patterned things. How to use those very simple things, bead tubes, to show off and dress up bigger, fancier beads. How a bead tube in one set of colors looks one way and how in another set of colors looks entirely different. I hope you have as much fun playing with bead tubes as I do. Along the way, I also hope you learn some useful things about beading. I always do. It's one of the things that keeps sewing one little bead to another little bead over and over and over again interesting and fascinating.

In This Book

In this book, you'll learn how to use peyote and brick stitch to make all kinds of fascinating and beautiful bead tubes. You can flip directly to the projects if you are an experienced beader, or turn to the Stitch How-tos section on p. 10 for a complete guide to the basics. All projects are made with just those two stitches, but the design possibilities are incredible!

I've also included two bonus sections: How to Read Charts and Odd-Count Peyote Turns. Both are important to making the bead tubes in this book and both can be difficult for some of us to learn. I wrote the How to Read Charts section because I have trouble reading charts. I set out to learn what caused me such problems. The first was that different designers assumed I was going to bead in the same directions as they did—top to bottom or left to right. If I didn't, then I immediately had difficulties. So the first thing was to figure out how the chart needed to look for the way I wanted to bead and then move the chart around so that I could. The second thing was I had a hard time keeping my place on the chart. You'll find some tips for that as well, although with whatever method you use, it gets easier with time and practice.

Odd-count peyote turns elicit groans every time I mention them in classes I teach. Most of us are familiar with only one, perhaps two, ways to do odd-count turns. One of them is usually a variation of the Woven or Figure-8 turn, which is unloved by nearly everybody. So I collected several other ways of doing odd count turns, a couple of which are really, really easy, so you should find one you like. The whole point is to add a bead at the end of the row and get the needle going in the opposite direction for the next row. Whatever works is good.

About Bead Tubes

Over my beading life, I've made many things—jewelry, pictures, and sculptures—but I always return to making tubes. Small tubes, short tubes, long tubes, tiny tubes, or big tubes are so versatile and so much fun to make.

A bead tube jewelry project can take an hour or it can take weeks. Short tubes can become earrings, a bracelet, or a necklace. A long tube can support a pendant or more tubes. Tubes can be sporty, elegant, gaudy, demure—whatever you want them to be.

A short project might need only one or two tubes and a couple of findings. A larger project might take a series of beading sessions to accumulate dozens of tubes for a more ambitious bracelet or necklace. All bead tube projects offer some instant gratification as each tube is completed. Some projects offer the satisfaction of making a complex project involving many tubes as well as the relief of—finally—completing it!

Have fun and enjoy making the jewelry in this book. Feel free to adapt your own color preferences or innovations for each project. One of the best things about beading is the ability to make your own unique version of any project. I think of new ideas every time I look at the projects in this book.

Happy beading!

–Nancy Zellers

Toolbox

Every beader needs a toolbox, whether it's a plain plastic box like mine or a treasured tin. In my toolbox, I keep all the things I need for most projects.

Stitching Tools

Needles: I normally use size 10 beading needles, about 2 in. (5 cm) long. Size 12 beading needles are useful when you are making many passes through a bead or the bead holes are quite small. I bend the finer size 12s easily, though, and find them much harder to thread. A beading sharp, a needle about 1¼ in. (3.2 cm) long, is useful for beading in tight corners.

Needle container: This container holds new and used needles. (Old, bent-up needles are useful for small beading tasks.) My container is large enough to hold needles securely on the magnetized surface, and it also holds a small pair of scissors, a pair of tweezers, and thread. It's a nice "take-along" rather than carrying the whole toolbox. An Altoids tin can easily be modified into a needle container.

Scissors: These should be very small, very sharp, and reserved for trimming nylon threads. Another pair of scissors should be used for Fireline and similar threads, as they dull a pair of scissors quickly and permanently. Good-quality scissors should be reserved for beading only.

Threads: I use Nymo nylon thread in sizes B and D. It is a durable parallel filament thread. It comes in many colors on small bobbins. I keep black and white in my toolbox. Another nylon beading thread is Silamide, which is a twisted filament thread. It looks like a tiny rope, and the cut end flares out like a frayed rope. It comes in two weights and few colors. Many people prefer to use it for heavy jewelry projects. It is stronger for the thread size than Nymo and somewhat less apt to fray.

When I'm working with crystal or metal beads, which may have sharp edges, I use Fireline, a gel-spun polyethylene (GSP) thread originally created as fishing line, in either a 6-lb. or 8-lb. test weight, and usually in the smoke color. I use the crystal (or white) Fireline only if the beads are white or very light colored. The smoke color disappears quite nicely with most beads. Fireline is stiffer and kinkier to work with and often makes clunkier knots than Nymo.

Use white thread for light-colored beads, as it keeps the colors bright and clear by not casting a shadow. A beige or gray thread may dull the colors. A black thread may darken the overall color of the bead work and absolutely kill the liveliness of the beads. Don't use black thread unless your beads are predominantly black. Colored threads, sometimes even matching colored thread, will show through transparent or translucent beads, which you might not like. White will normally disappear. If white thread shows on the ends of the finished bead tubes, color the white thread with a permanent marker to match the beads. To color the thread, put the broad tip of the marker on top of the thread and slowly pull the thread under it. You may need to do it a couple of times to get an even color. Work on a piece of plastic or foil so you don't color your work surface, too!

Thread conditioners: I normally don't condition the thread. I find the coating on the thread is sufficient. However, conditioner adds a slickness to the thread and can help prevent tangles. In that case, use Thread Heaven, which is a conditioner that helps prevent fraying, strengthens the thread, creates a slick coating, and imparts a slight static charge to reduce tangling. Another thread conditioner is beeswax or synthetic beeswax. It is good for making the thread stiffer, stickier, and thicker. It helps keep the threads together if you are working with doubled thread. I rarely use wax and

notebook

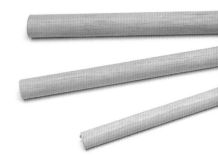

only for a specific need. Wax is very difficult to use with brick stitch, although it is OK with peyote stitch when needed.

Thread burner: This battery-operated device heats up quickly to a high temperature. It cuts and seals nylon threads and gets rid of pesky short ends and fuzzy fibers. Not a necessity, but nice to have.

Tweezers: Choose a flat-tipped pair of tweezers for pulling needles through beads and other tasks, and a very pointy-tipped pair for undoing tangles and knots. Insert the points of the tweezers in the center of the knot and let them gently open. This often pries the knot apart so you can finish pulling the threads back into order.

Ruler: A 6-in. (15 cm) ruler fits in the toolbox. A cloth tape measure is also handy for measuring necklaces or for measuring wrists and necks for sizing.

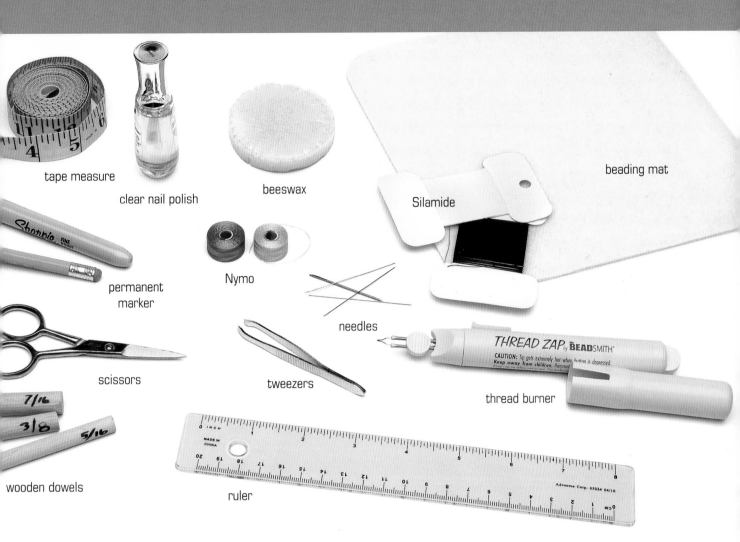

tape measure

clear nail polish

beeswax

Silamide

beading mat

Sharpie FINE POINT

permanent marker

Nymo

needles

THREAD ZAP by BEADSMITH
CAUTION: Tip gets extremely hot when button is depressed.
Keep away from children, flammable

scissors

tweezers

thread burner

7/16

3/8

5/16

wooden dowels

ruler

0 INCH 1 2 3 4 5 6 7 8
MADE IN CHINA
Advantus Corp. 65024 04/10

Bead scoop: This long, narrow, curved piece of metal is used to pick up and repackage beads or rearrange them on the bead mat. A triangle sorter also works well. I don't find the tiny shovel scoops nearly as useful.

Wooden dowels: You may need several of them about 6 in. long in various diameters from ⅛–⅝ in. (3–16 cm) to use as supports for tubular beading.

Clear nail polish: Seals knots or coats threads attaching clasps or jump rings. Wipe the tip of an old needle across the nail polish brush and then across the knot. Avoid getting the polish on your beads, especially if they are matte beads! Sometimes you can just carefully dab at the knot or threads with the brush.

Beading mat or surface: I use Vellux pads, readily available from bead stores, in a light beige or ivory color. They have a soft surface so beads don't bounce

around, they don't catch the needle tip, are washable, and fold or roll up for transport and storage. If you're working with white or beige or very light-colored beads, use a dark mat.

The mat on my beading table is quite large and fits in a tray I carry around with my beading project on it. Another small one is cut to fit my toolbox, and still another provides padding for fragile pieces and doubles as a beading mat when needed. Sometimes you can lay another pad on top of the one you are using and roll the two together tightly to keep the beads in place. I normally just scoop up the beads and put them back into their containers for transport.

Pencil/pen and notebook: Be sure to take quick notes about the project or supplies if necessary.

Permanent marker: A small black marker for coloring the last ½ in.

(1.3 cm) of thread tips makes it easier to thread the needle. You can also use it for marking beads.

Toolbox or container: I like to use a 5 x 8 in. (13 x 20 cm) plastic food storage box with a snap-down lid. Everything fits in it and, with the secure lid, I can just throw it in a bag or box along with my current beading project. I've seen pretty tin containers, some neat lunch boxes, and many other interesting and innovative toolboxes.

Plastic bags: I use various sizes to contain the materials for a project: the instructions, beads, thread, findings and partially completed beadwork. Plastic boxes also work well.

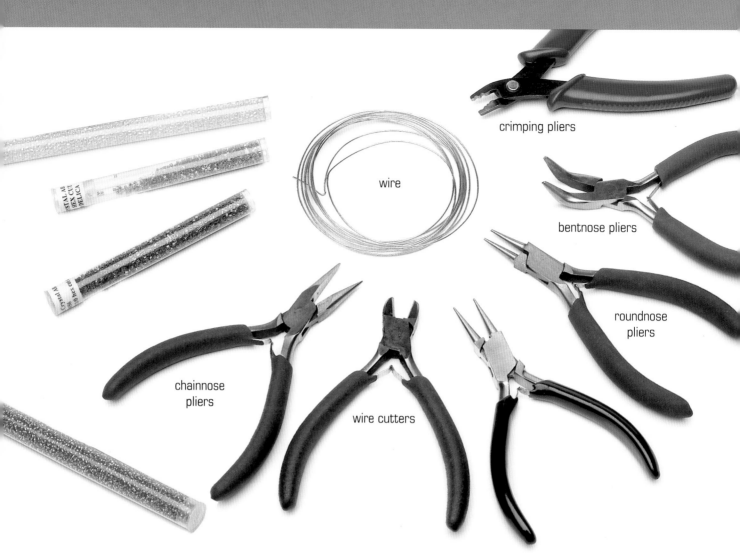

crimping pliers

wire

bentnose pliers

roundnose pliers

chainnose pliers

wire cutters

Ott-Lite or other full-spectrum light: This portable true-color light has a bulb that stays cool. You can match bead and thread colors under a Ott-Lite. I've found I can bead longer as the light is easier on my eyes. The cool bulb means that your hands don't get hot working under the light. Some models come with attached magnifiers, although I prefer the separate Mag-Eyes for more freedom of movement. Carry a handy extension cord along with your portable light.

Mag-Eyes: This lightweight magnifying system is wearable over your regular glasses or contacts and has several lenses of different strengths. Mine travel in their own plastic box along with an extra beading mat.

A small trash bin: On my beading table, it is a small plastic wastebasket in a bright lime green. Away from home, it is frequently a paper cup or a small plastic bag that I can throw away later.

Metal board and magnetic strips: These are very useful when working charts, because the magnetic strips hold the paper to the board. The moveable strips will keep your place, row by row, as you bead. When you move or store the project, the magnetic strips stay in place so you know where to restart.

Bead storage: Everyone has her own system and preferences. I keep my beads in plastic tubes and glass jars, frequently baby food jars. The tubes and jars are sorted into plastic shoe boxes by color and sometimes by size, depending on how many I have in a particular color range. I rarely keep beads in plastic bags as sooner or later the plastic bag will split open, spilling loose beads into the bottom of the shoe box. The shoe boxes are arranged on open shelving so I can find what I'm looking for easily.

Pliers and cutters: To assemble most jewelry, you'll need some pliers and wire

cutters along with the specific findings (beading wire, clasps, ear wires, and so on) for that project. Most often, you'll need chainnose pliers, roundnose pliers, and a flush wire cutter. I like to have two pairs of curved chainnose pliers or bentnose pliers when I'm opening jump rings so I can see the jump ring, the components, and my progress easily.

A useful purchase is a pair of crimping pliers. They are a specialized tool for folding crimp beads when assembling jewelry. You can use chainnose pliers, but crimping pliers do a much better job.

You can buy sets of pliers, although the set seldom includes crimping pliers. Buy good quality tools; they are much easier to work with, and you'll get better results.

Findings

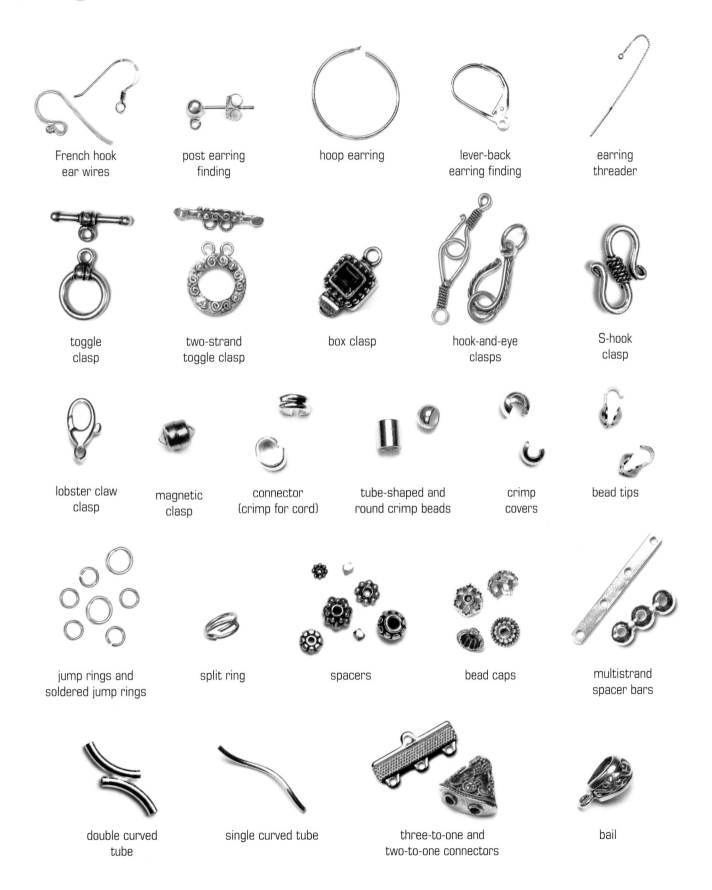

French hook
ear wires

post earring
finding

hoop earring

lever-back
earring finding

earring
threader

toggle
clasp

two-strand
toggle clasp

box clasp

hook-and-eye
clasps

S-hook
clasp

lobster claw
clasp

magnetic
clasp

connector
(crimp for cord)

tube-shaped and
round crimp beads

crimp
covers

bead tips

jump rings and
soldered jump rings

split ring

spacers

bead caps

multistrand
spacer bars

double curved
tube

single curved tube

three-to-one and
two-to-one connectors

bail

Stitch How-tos

Peyote Stitch
Even-count Flat Peyote

1 String a stop bead (p. 13) and pass through it again.

2 String an even number of beads (here, 10). This string of beads becomes the first and second rows.

3 String one bead (Bead 11) and pass back through the next-to-last bead strung in step 2 (Bead 9). The new bead will sit on top of the last bead of the first row (Bead 10).

4 String one bead (Bead 12), skip a bead (Bead 8) and pass through the next bead (Bead 7). Notice how the new bead pushes the bead below it down about a half bead, starting the characteristic up/down of peyote stitch.

5 String a bead (Bead 13), skip a bead (Bead 6), and pass through the next bead (Bead 5).

6 Continue stringing one bead, skipping a bead, and passing through the next bead to the end of the row.

7 To start the next row, string one bead (Bead 16) and pass through the up-bead (Bead 15).

8 Continue across the row, filling in between each up-bead with a new bead.

9 Repeat steps 6 and 7 for the length of the piece.

10 When you are finished with the beadwork, remove the stop bead.

TIP Here are three easy ways to count peyote rows:

• Using the chart at right, and starting with a green bead, zig-zag your way up the green column and the adjacent white column. Here, there are 10 beads in each column for a total of 20.

• Count the beads on each edge of the beadwork (here, all the red beads and all the green beads; 20 again).

• Just count the beads on one edge and multiply by two. While you are stitching, be sure you are exiting on the right-hand side before you count.

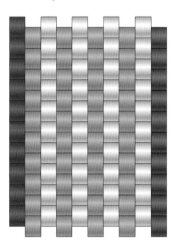

Even-count Tubular Peyote

Even-count tubular peyote makes horizontal stepped rings around the tube. Each row shifts one bead to the left from the previous row and requires a step-up to start the next row.

1 String an even number of beads and tie the beads into a circle. Placing the bead circle around a support can be helpful.

2 Pass through the bead to the left of the knot (a) and begin adding beads as you would for flat peyote: String a bead, skip a bead, and sew through the next bead.

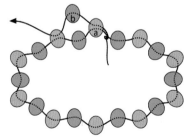

3 Each time a row ends, go through the last bead of the previous row (a) and the first bead of the current row (b). This is the step-up.

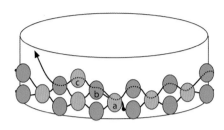

4 String a bead (c) and continue adding beads in between the up-beads.

Odd-count Tubular Peyote

Odd-count tubular peyote stitch produces a continuous spiral. It does not require a step-up.

1 String an odd number of beads and tie into a circle. Use a support, like a pen or a dowel, if you wish.

2 Pass through the bead to the left of the knot and beginning adding beads as you would for flat peyote: String a bead, skip a bead, and sew through the next bead.

3 Work continuously around the tube filling in between the up-beads for the length desired.

Odd-Count Flat Peyote

Many beaders avoid odd-count peyote turns because they seem difficult and confusing. However, odd-count peyote lets you make designs that are centered, so it is a very worthwhile technique to master. Most of us only know one or two odd-count turns, usually the unloved Figure-8 or Woven turn. Once you find a technique that you like, you'll be able to make centered designs comfortably.

Here are seven ways to do odd-count turns to get you started: two woven ones and five others. Try them all. The Two-needle Odd-count Turn is probably the fastest technique once you get the hang of it, and it has the least amount of thread on the turning edge.

Odd-count flat peyote is stitched just like even-count, except on every other row, you have to make a special odd-count turn.

There is no single right way to do an odd-count turn. The whole point is to add a bead at the end of the row and get the needle going in the opposite direction for the next row. Whatever works is fine. Experiment with these turns and your own inventions to find the best method for you.

TIP Consider using one of the Woven Turns for the initial odd-count turn (unless you're stitching with two needles). These two sturdy woven stitches lock in the first beads in a project and make it easy to use one of the other turns for the rest of the piece.

TIP Remember that you make odd-count turns only every other row. The starting side of the beadwork has an odd-count turn; the other side has a normal peyote turn.

TIP Complete the odd-count peyote turn before you even start thinking about working the next row. Many of us get confused about whether we are adding the last bead of the current row or the first bead of the next row. This tip will help you keep it straight in your mind.

Woven Turn 1 (or Figure-8 Turn)
The traditional figure-8 turns for odd-count peyote make a thicker and stiffer edge which you may occasionally prefer.

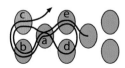

String the first two rows and work the third row as you normally would for peyote. Just before the end of the row (exiting bead e):

1 Pass diagonally through the first two beads (a and b) on the previous rows.
2 String the last bead (c) for the current row.
3 Pass diagonally downward through two beads (a and d) in the previous rows.
4 Pass through the bead directly above the last bead exited (e) and diagonally downward through the next two beads (a and b) on the previous rows.
5 Pass through the last bead added (c) and peyote back across the row.

Woven Turn 2
Here is a slightly different way of doing a figure-8 turn. String the first two rows and work them as you normally would for peyote. At the end of the row (exiting bead c):

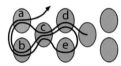

1 String the last bead (a) for this row.
2 Pass through bead directly below (b) and diagonally upwards through the next two beads (c and d) on the previous rows.
3 Pass through the bead directly below (e) and the next two beads in the previous rows (c and b).
4 Pass through the last bead added (a) and peyote back across the row.

Looped Turn
This easy-turn method is one of my favorites.

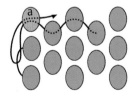

String the first two rows and work the third row as you normally would for peyote. At the end of the row:

First turn:
1 String the last bead of the row.
2 Tie the tail thread and working thread together. (Note that this leaves a knot, which may not be desirable.)

3 Pass back through the last bead added and work peyote stitch across the row. You can also work a woven turn for the first row.

Subsequent turns:
1 String the last bead of the row (a).
2 Pass the needle under the loop of thread connecting the end beads of the previous rows.
3 Pass back through the last bead added (a) and work peyote stitch across the row.

Easy One-Bead Turn
This is a simple odd-count turn. String the first two rows and work the third row as you normally would for even-count peyote. Just before the end of the row (exiting bead a):

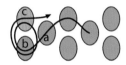

1 Pass through the last bead on the first row (b).
2 String one bead to become the last bead of the current row (c).
3 Pass through the last bead on the row directly below (b) again.
4 Pass through the last bead added (c) and work peyote stitch across the row.

Wraparound Turn
This one-bead turn with a loop around previous thread is a bit complicated but works well. String the first two rows and work the third row as you normally would for peyote. At the end of the row:

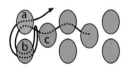

1 String the last bead (a).
2 Pass through the bead directly below the bead just added (b).
3 Loop the working thread around the thread between the bead on the row above (c) and the last bead added (a). Pass back through the bead you just exited (b).

4 Pass through the last bead added (a) and work peyote back across the row.

Tail Thread Turn

Suitable for short pieces of work, the tail thread turn solves that pesky tail thread problem! It adds a long thread to the left edge of the beadwork. Be sure it is well anchored so it doesn't snag and pull out. String the first two rows and work the third row as you normally would for peyote. At the end of the row:

1 String the last bead of the row (a).
2 Loop the working thread around the tail thread, pulling it up and alongside the edge of the beads. Pull the working thread snug and keep the tail thread pulled tight to the edge of the beads.
3 Pass back through the last bead added (a) and continue working peyote across the row.

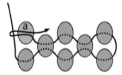

Two-needle Turn

If you are a fan of two-needle beadweaving or would just like to try out a two-needle odd-count peyote turn, here it is.

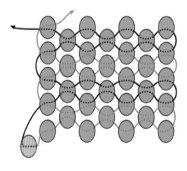

1 Put a stop bead (red) in the middle of your thread. String the first two rows of beads (green) on the right-hand thread.
2 Using the right-hand (working) thread, work the next row of peyote, returning to the starting side of the beadwork. String the last bead for this row and slide it into place at the end of the row.
3 Put down the working thread, pick up the idle thread on the left to become the working thread (black), and remove the stop bead. Pass back through the last bead added with the working thread. Pull on both threads in opposite directions to

snug the bead into place at the end of the row. Work the rest of the row with the new working thread.
4 Use the same thread to work back across on the next row. String the last bead for this row and slide it into place at the end of the row.
5 Put down the working thread. Pick up the idle thread. Pass back through the last bead added, pull it into place, and work the rest of the row.

Brick Stitch
Flat Brick Stitch

1 Start a ladder of beads by stringing two beads. Slide the beads near the end of the thread. Pass the needle back through the first bead in the same direction. Position the two beads so they sit flat, side by side. Pass through the second bead. Continue stringing one bead and passing through the previous bead and the bead just added until your ladder is the length desired. Notice that the loop of thread between the beads changes direction each time from clockwise to counter-clockwise and back again. Position the ladder so it exits upward from the last bead.

2 Start the next row by stringing two beads. Pass the needle under the loop of thread connecting the last two beads on the previous row. Settle the new beads parallel to the previous row and side-by-side with each other. Pass back up through the second (inside) bead of the pair.

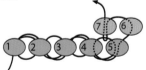

3 Continue the row by stringing one bead, looping under the thread between the next pair of beads on the previous row, and passing back up through the new bead. Repeat to the end of the row.
4 Repeat steps 2 and 3 for the length of the piece.

Tubular Brick Stitch

1 Make a ladder (Step 1 of Flat Brick Stitch) the length needed.

2 Connect the beginning and ending beads of the ladder by sewing through both beads. Be careful not to twist the ladder as you do so.
3 Position the circle of beads so the thread is exiting upward by turning the bead circle over or passing through one of the beads to position the thread, if necessary.
4 Follow steps 2 and 3 in the Flat Brick Stitch instructions to make the next row.
5 At the end of the row, connect the beginning and ending beads by passing down through the first bead of the row. Loop under the thread bridge below it and back up through the same bead.
6 Repeat steps 4 and 5 for the length of the tube.

Two-drop Stitches
Two-drop Ladder

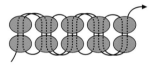

Start a ladder of beads by stringing four beads. Pass the needle back through the first two beads in the same direction. Position the four beads so they sit side by side in two stacks of two. Pass through the second stack of beads. Continue by stringing two beads and passing through the previous bead stack and through the two-bead stack just added for the length desired. Join the ends if working tubular brick stitch.

Two-drop Peyote

Work two-drop peyote stitch the same as basic peyote, but treat pairs of beads as if they were single beads.

Start by stringing an even number of beads divisible by four. Pick up two beads (stitch 1 of row 3), skip two beads, and go through the next two beads. Repeat across the row.

Two-drop Brick

1 Start a row of two-drop brick stitch by stringing four beads. Pass the needle under the loop of the thread connecting two beads in the previous row. Settle the new beads parallel to the previous row and side by side with each other in two stacks of two. Pass back up through the second (inside) stack of beads.

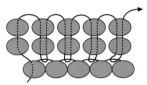

2 Continue by stringing two beads, looping under the thread between the next pair of beads on the previous row and back up through the new stack of beads. Repeat to the end of the row. Connect the last and first stitches if working tubular brick stitch.

Other Beading Techniques
Stop Bead

For a stop bead, use a bead of a different size or color or both from those you will be using for the project. Add it to the thread first, sliding it to 6–8 in. (15–20 cm) from the end. Pass the needle through the bead again in the same direction. This puts a loop of thread around the bead but lets you slide it up and down the thread easily. Its purpose is to keep the beads from falling off as you are picking up the first rows of the project and also to give you a little bit of resistance while you work the first row of beading.

Overhand knot

Make a loop at the end of the thread. Pull the short tail through the loop, and tighten.

Half-hitch knot
Pass the needle under the thread between two beads. A loop will form as you pull the thread through. Cross over the thread between the beads, sew through the loop, and pull gently to draw the knot into the beadwork.

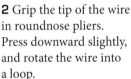

Square knot
1 Bring the left-hand thread over the right-hand thread, and bring it under and back up.
2 Cross right over left, go through the loop, and pull both ends.

Ending and Adding Thread
To end a thread, weave back into the beadwork, following the existing thread path and tying two or three half-hitch knots around thread between beads as you go. Change directions as you weave so the thread crosses itself. Sew through a few beads after the last knot before cutting the thread. To add a thread, start several rows below the point where the last bead was added, and weave through the beadwork, tying half-hitch knots between beads.

Zipping up
To join two sections of a flat peyote piece invisibly, match up the two pieces so the edge beads fit together. "Zip up" the pieces by zigzagging through the up-beads on both edges.

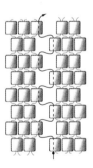

Crimping
1 Position the crimp bead in the hole of the crimping pliers that is closest to the handle.
2 Holding the wires apart, squeeze the tool to compress the crimp bead, making sure one wire is on each side of the dent.
3 Place the crimp bead in the front hole of the tool, and position it so the dent is facing outward. Squeeze the tool to fold the crimp in half.
4 Tug on the wires to ensure that the crimp is secure.

To simply flatten a crimp bead, squeeze it tightly with chainnose pliers.

Plain loops
1 Using chainnose pliers, make a right-angle bend about ¼ in. (6 mm) from the end of the wire.
2 Grip the tip of the wire in roundnose pliers. Press downward slightly, and rotate the wire into a loop.
3 Let go, then grip the loop at the same place on the pliers, and keep turning to close the loop. The closer to the tip of the roundnose pliers that you work, the smaller the loop will be.

Wrapped loops

1 Using chainnose pliers, make a right-angle bend approximately 1¼ in. (3.2 cm) from the end of the wire.

2 Position the jaws of your roundnose pliers in the bend.

3 Curve the short end of the wire over the top jaw of the roundnose pliers.

4 Reposition the pliers so the lower jaw fits snugly in the loop. Curve the wire downward around the bottom jaw of the pliers. This is the first half of a wrapped loop.

5 To complete the wraps, grasp the top of the loop with chainnose pliers.

6 Wrap the wire around the stem two or three times. Trim the excess wire, and gently press the cut end close to the wraps with chainnose pliers.

Opening and closing loops or jump rings

1 Hold the loop or jump ring with two pairs of chainnose pliers or chainnose and round-nose pliers, as shown.

2 To open the loop or jump ring, bring one pair of pliers toward you and push the other pair away. String materials on the open loop or jump ring. Reverse the steps to close the open loop or jump ring.

Reading Charts

The key for any peyote or brick stitch chart is to move the chart around so you can bead as you want. You'll find charts positioned in different ways depending on that designer's preferred method.

I'm going to show you four different ways to read both peyote and brick charts. I'll start by showing you how to read a chart beaded from left to right, then I'll go through three other ways to use the chart. From those examples, you should be able to figure out how to move a chart around for your beading preference. Watch for the key element in each type of chart to help you. A copier or computer can be a helpful tool for enlarging charts changing their positioning.

Keep in mind that this is how you *read* a chart. You may actually hold the beadwork differently in your hand. Whenever you need to check if you are working the chart correctly, reposition your beadwork so it matches the chart.

Flat Peyote Charts

Flat peyote charts can be read bottom up (bottom to top) or top down (top to bottom). And left to right or right to left. The key is to position the chart the way you want to read it. I usually read charts bottom up, left to right, so let's start there.

Even-count peyote
Bottom up/Left to right

1 Position the chart so the first column (red) sticks up and the last column (green) hangs down. For even-count peyote, the starting bead position should stick up and the last bead on the row should hang down.
2 Pick up beads for first two rows, left to right (red, blue, white, blue, white, and so on, ending with green).
3 Now you are ready to start adding beads for the third row, beginning with the second green bead from the bottom.
4 Read the chart from right to left, picking up that green bead to start, then blue beads for the rest of the row.
5 The red bead, second from the bottom, will start your fourth row. After adding the red bead, you'll add white beads between each of the blue beads, reading back across the chart from left to right.

Even-count peyote
Top down/Right to left

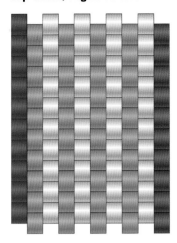

Using the same chart position, start picking up beads for the first two rows at the top, starting with the green column and reading right to left. Start the third row by picking up the red bead (second from top) and working across the row left to right. Continue reading down the chart.

Even-count peyote
Bottom up/Right to left

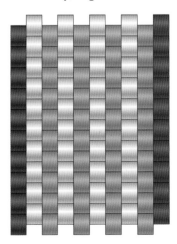

This chart is flipped on a vertical axis 180 degrees to create a mirror image of the chart that shows bottom up, left to right. You can scan your chart into a computer and then flip it so that the red column is on the right, sticking up, and the green column is on the left, hanging down. Many software programs have a setting called "mirror image." Copy shops can do it for you as well.

Start by picking up beads for the first two rows, starting with the bottom red bead and picking up the beads from right to left.

Even-count Peyote
Top down/Left to right

Using the same chart position as the bottom-up/right to left even-count peyote, start picking up beads on the top two rows, starting with the green column on the left and reading from left to right.

Odd-count Peyote
Bottom up/Either direction

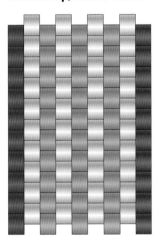

Notice that both the red and green bottom edge beads are hanging down. You can start on either edge. Your odd-count turn is always on the edge where you started (the tail thread edge). On that side, you add the edge bead as the last bead in the row. Use the next column, a white bead in this chart, as the start of the next row.

Odd-count peyote
Top down/Either direction

Both of the edge beads stick up at the top. You can work in either direction. Remember to use the second column (a white bead) as the start of subsequent rows on the odd-turn edge. To position the chart for odd-count peyote, top down, you will need to use the computer to flip the bottom-up chart on a horizontal axis.

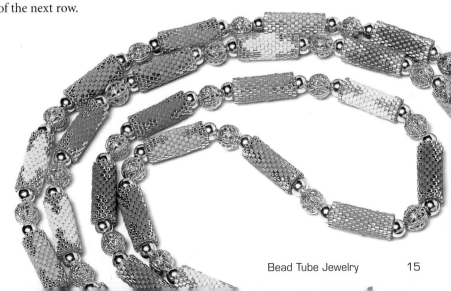

Tubular Peyote Charts

Reading a chart for even-count tubular peyote is different from flat peyote. You read in the same direction for each row and you need to do a step-up or step-down at the end of each row. You can read tubular charts bottom up or top down and right to left (clockwise) or left to right (counterclockwise). Again, the trick is to position the chart for the way you want to work. I usually work tubular peyote bottom up and clockwise, so we'll start there. Remember, this is about reading the chart. How you are holding the beadwork in your hand may be different.

Even-count tubular peyote
Bottom up/Right to left (clockwise)

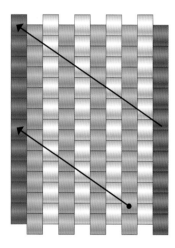

1 Position the chart so the left column (red) sticks up and the right column (green) hangs down.
2 Pick up beads for the first two rows, right to left (green, white, blue, white, blue, and so on, ending with red.
3 Tie the beads into a circle so the green bead is to the left of the knot.
4 Go through the green bead and the next white bead.
5 You are now ready to start the third row with a blue bead. Many tubular charts will have a diagonal line on the chart indicating the way the designer beaded the project and wants you to read the chart. You'll notice the diagonal line starts in the third row two columns over from the right edge. This diagonal line shows you the first bead of each row on

this chart. If necessary, you can draw your own diagonal line.
6 At the end of the row on the chart, skip back to the right edge on the same row. When you reach the starting bead (white), go through it and the first bead added (blue)—the step-up required by even-count tubular peyote. The next bead (white) starts the fourth row.

Did you notice that each new row starts one bead to the left of the previous row?

Even-count tubular peyote
Top down/Left to right (counterclockwise)

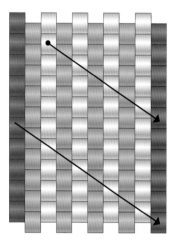

This is the same chart position as for bottom up, clockwise.
1 Pick up beads for the first two rows, left to right (red, blue, white, blue, white, and so on, ending with green).
2 Tie the beads into a circle so the red bead is to the right of the knot.
3 Go through the red bead and the next blue bead.
4 You are now ready to start the third row with a white bead. Notice the diagonal line has the same slant as the bottom up, clockwise chart. You are just starting on the other end of the chart.
5 At the end of the of the row on the chart, skip back to the left edge on the same row.
6 When you reach the starting blue bead, go through it and the first white bead added—the step-down required by even-count tubular peyote. A blue bead starts the fourth row.

Did you notice that each new row starts one bead to the right of the previous row when beading counterclockwise?

Even-Count Tubular Peyote
Top down/Right to left (clockwise)

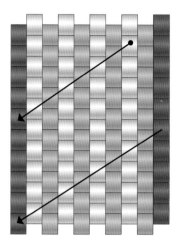

The chart has been repositioned so the start bead is on the right and sticking up. It is a mirror image of the bottom up, clockwise chart.

On this chart, the red bead will be to the left of the knot and you'll shift left to start each row.

Even-count Tubular Peyote
Bottom up/Left to right (counterclockwise)

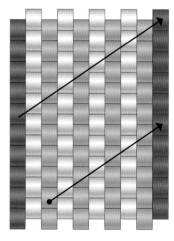

This is the same chart as the one above. Just starting picking up your beads from the bottom left. On this chart, the green bead will be to the right of the knot and you'll shift right to start each row.

Odd-Count Tubular Peyote

What about odd-count tubular peyote? Odd-count tubular peyote works great for solid-color tubes or for spiraling tubes, but you don't often see it used with a pattern. While it is possible to design a project with an odd-count tubular peyote pattern, it is much easier to use even-count tubular peyote.

Flat Brick Stitch

Flat brick stitch charts are easier to read than peyote charts. You can read bottom up or top down and left to right or right to left. Again, it is a matter of positioning the chart for the way you want to use it.

The first row in brick stitch is the ladder row. (For these instructions, the ladder row defines the direction of beading.) The second row is the important one for us. Watch the position of the red bead. The key is to get the first bead of the second row where you want it: It should be sticking out.

Flat brick stitch
Bottom up/Left to right

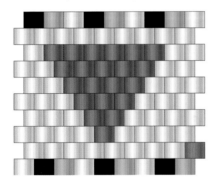

Bead your first row, the ladder row, from left to right. The second row starts with the red bead. Pick up beads from right to left. For the first stitch, you pick up the red bead plus a white one. After that the rest of the row is one bead at a time. The third row starts on the left edge again.

Flat brick stitch
Top down/Right to Left

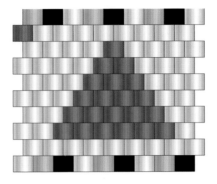

This chart is the same as the previous bottom up, left to right chart, turned 180 degrees. Pick up the ladder row from right to left and begin the second row with the red bead on the left side.

Flat Brick Stitch
Bottom up/Right to left

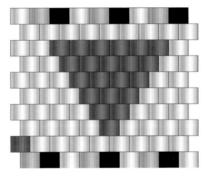

This chart is flipped to create a mirror image of the bottom up, left to right one. You'll start with the bottom row, working right to left.

Flat brick stitch
Top down/Left to right

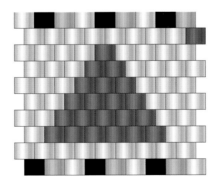

This is the bottom up, right to left chart above turned 180 degrees. Pick up the ladder row from left to right and start the second row with the red bead on the right.

TIP Tubular brick stitch can be worked flat and then the edges can be zipped together to make the tube. Occasionally, it is best to work a tubular stitch, such as when the bead sizes are different or irregular.

Tubular Brick Charts

When reading a brick stitch chart for a tubular pattern, it is easiest to start in the center of a row rather than on one edge. In these charts, one bead in the ladder row is red to show our starting place for the second row of each chart.

Tubular brick stitch
Bottom up/Left to right (counterclockwise)

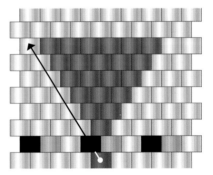

1 Make the ladder row, working from either direction, connecting the first and last beads of the row. Then work your needle to the red bead with the thread exiting the top of the bead.
2 From the middle of the second row, just over the red bead, pick up the black and blue beads. Go under the loop between the red bead and the white bead to the right and back through the blue bead.
3 Continue, picking up beads to the right each time. At the end of the row on the chart, skip back to the beginning of the row on the left edge.

4 After adding the last bead in the row (white), connect it to the first bead (black) by going down through the black bead and back up through the same bead, catching the loop on the row below.

5 Start the third row by picking up the white and green beads. Notice the diagonal line on the chart: The starting bead for the third row has shifted one bead to the left from the second row. This shift will occur on each new row.

Tubular brick stitch
Bottom up/Right to left (clockwise)

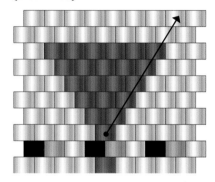

1 Make the ladder row, connecting the first and last beads of the row. Then work your needle to the red bead, exiting the top of the bead.

2 From the middle of the second row, just over the red bead, pick up the blue and black beads. Go under the loop between the red bead and the white bead to the left and back through the black bead.

3 Continue, picking up beads to the left each time. At the end of the row on the chart, skip back to the beginning of the row on the right edge.

4 After adding the last bead in the row (white), connect it to the first bead (blue) by going down through the blue bead and back through the same bead.

5 Start the third row by picking up the white and green beads. See the diagonal line on the chart. Notice that the starting bead for the third row has shifted one bead to the right from the second row.

Tubular brick stitch
Top down/Either direction

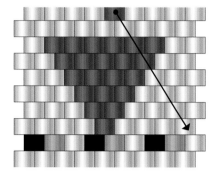

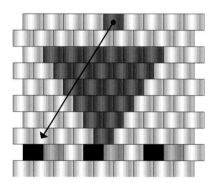

If you prefer to work top down, the same shift to the left or right applies on each row depending on the direction you are stitching. See the diagonal lines on the charts above. In this case, I didn't even reposition the chart from bottom up. I just started with a center bead at the top of the chart instead. If you prefer, you can flip the original chart.

Read a Peyote Chart as Brick Stitch and Vice Versa

Now that you know how to read both peyote and brick stitch charts, did you know that you can read any peyote or brick chart as the other stitch? For example, here's an even-count peyote chart:

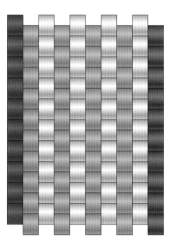

Let's bead it in brick stitch by turning the chart so the rows run horizontally instead of vertically.

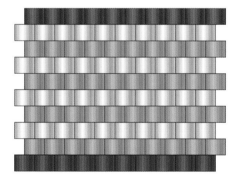

And you can continue repositioning the chart until you can bead it your favorite way! These are arranged for a bottom-up, left-to-right style.

What about odd-count charts? Here's the odd count flat peyote chart:

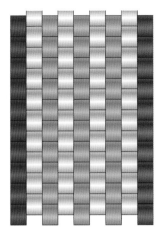

Let's make it a brick stitch chart:

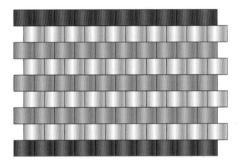

I hope this helps you understand how to read bead charts and how to position a chart for your beading preference. However the designer does the chart, you can rearrange it. Have fun making charted beadwork—some of the most exciting designs in the bead world to me!

"Where am I?" How do you keep track of which row you are beading? For brick stitch, it's easy. Just lay a straight-edge or piece of paper under the row you are currently working. Move it up (or down) as you complete each row. I like to make a small check mark on the edge of the chart as well. If the straight-edge gets jostled and moved out of position, it's easier to find my stopping place.

For peyote stitch, it is a little more difficult. Peyote rows move upward (or downward) one-half bead per row. So when you are beading a row, you are looking for the "whole" beads and ignoring the "half" beads. Lay a straight-edge across a chart and you'll see that it is positioned under some beads and divides others in half. It takes some practice to train your eye to see just the whole beads and ignore the half beads.

Here's the way I handle that problem:

1 Make two photocopies of your chart, enlarging them if you want.
2 Cut across the middle of one of the charts following the ups and downs of the beads. This makes a comb shape.
3 Turn the comb over so the blank side of the paper is up. You can use markers to make this black or some other color if you want.
4 Lay the comb on top of the other copy of the chart. Position it so whole beads are centered in the downs or slots of the comb. The ups or teeth will be covering the half beads. Now you can easily see which beads to string for each row.
5 When you finish a row, move the comb up one-half bead and to the left or right one column. Now the beads for that row are centered in the downs.

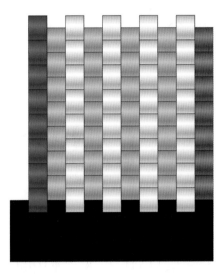

I use a metal board and magnetic strips to keep the comb positioned on the chart and usually check off each row as I finish it in case my comb gets moved out of position.

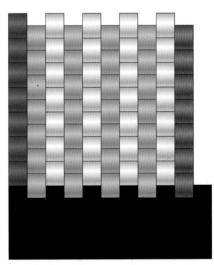

Tips for Making Bead Tubes

Begin with a Good Length of Thread

Thread your needle with a comfortable length of thread. The bead tubes do not take large amounts of thread. I usually start with an arm's length of thread, or what stretches between my hands when I hold them out at shoulder level. For me, that's about four feet.

Choose a Stitch

The bead tubes in this book are made with peyote or brick stitch. The charts are positioned for bottom up, left to right beading with peyote stitch. To make most beads, you can use flat peyote and zip up the edges. It is usually the best choice for patterned beads. You can make the beads with tubular peyote or with brick stitch, if you prefer. Some projects work best in tubular brick or odd-count tubular peyote, and the instructions will say so.

Bead Tube Supports

When working tubular peyote or tubular brick stitch, I often work around a support stick like a wooden dowel or a pencil—something that is about the same diameter as the bead tube. It helps me get the tube started and provides something to hang on to while I'm making the bead. Other beaders hate using supports, so try it both ways and decide which works best for you.

Bead Tube Fillers

Bead tubes, except very narrow ones, usually need a filling to keep them from collapsing. Two fillers that I use for short bead tubes are translucent plastic drinking straws and small plastic or glass beads.

Slit the plastic straws lengthwise and trim them to be slightly shorter than

the length of the bead tube. Squeeze the straw so the cut edges overlap, slide it into the bead tube, and let go. The straw will expand to fill the space.

One drawback of the straws is that they don't keep the stringing material centered in the bead tube. Sometimes it doesn't matter, as there are beads at each of the bead tube that partially block the ends and keep the beading wire centered. When you need to keep the bead tube centered on the beading wire or eye pin, consider using small beads to fill the interior of the bead tube. I prefer plastic beads because they are lighter than glass beads. Often an 8° seed bead is just right to fit inside a bead tube.

Some long tubes, like those for necklaces, may need a filler to keep them from collapsing where they curve around your neck or support a pendant. Work the tube around a narrow piece of satin rattail or other soft cord. Put the tube on a generous length of cord when it is an inch or two long (t is nearly impossible to pull a cord through a long tube after it is completed). A knot in each end of the cord will keep it from slithering through the tube unexpectedly. If you forget or the cord slithers out, try dropping a threaded needle down through the straightened tube. Then sew or tie the bead thread to the cord and pull it carefully through the tube. Trim the cord to fit when you are finished and secure it inside the tube with a couple of stitches from side to side before you add the clasps.

Now that you know how to create bead tubes in many different ways, let's begin!

Bead Tube
Jewelry

Dotted Swiss Bracelet

I remember the dotted Swiss dress
I had as a little girl—a pink-and-white one, all stiff
with starch—with a little straw bonnet and black
patent leather Mary Janes. I loved the dress
so much I had one when I was older too, which
probably wasn't all that good an idea. Now I just
reminisce with this bracelet.

1 Working in flat peyote stitch and following the chart, make two beads of each pastel color, accented by the pearl beads.

2 Cut 12 in. (30 cm) of beading wire. String one crimp bead. Slide the crimp near the end of the beading wire. Pass the end of the beading wire through one of the loops on the clasp and back through the crimp bead. Pull snug. Crimp. Repeat for the other bead strand.

3 On one beading strand, string one 6 mm pearl bead, one 8 mm pearl bead, and one bead tube. Alternate 8 mm pearl beads and bead tubes until all five bead tubes are strung. String one 8 mm pearl bead, one 6 mm pearl bead, and a crimp bead. String half of the clasp, and go back through the crimp bead and a few more beads. Pull snug. Crimp. Trim the excess beading wire.

4 Repeat for the other bead strand, matching the color order of the bead tubes on the first strand.

You'll need:

bracelet, 6½ in. (16.5 cm)
- 11º cylinder beads, 3 g each:
  - mint
  - purple
  - pale yellow
  - sapphire
  - rose
- 4 g 11º cylinder beads, pearl
- 12 8 mm pearl beads
- 4 6 mm pearl beads
- 4 crimp beads
- beading wire, .019
- clasp
- straws or filler beads
- white beading thread
- needle
- scissors
- chainnose or crimping pliers
- wire cutters

Voila! Earrings

Going somewhere? Need a gift? Have a new outfit that needs earrings? Make a short tube in your favorite colors, mix in a couple of beads in gold or silver, and hang from an ear wire or a decorative post. Voila! You've got a new pair of earrings to match your outfit.

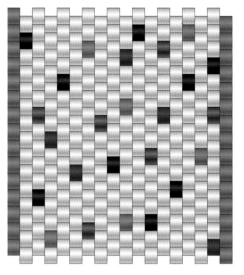

Confetti

Hanukkah

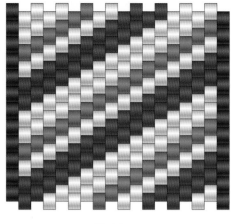

Christmas

confetti earrings

1 Follow the chart using white thread and peyote stitch. Zip the ends together.

2 Attach a gold thread to the bead tube, exiting through one of the gold edge beads.

3 String three gold beads and pass through the next edge bead in the same direction to make a loop. Repeat around both edges of the earring.

4 On a head pin, string a 2.5 mm round gold bead, an 8 mm round black bead, a bead tube, and an 8 mm round gold bead.

5 Make a loop at the top of the head pin. Attach to the ear wire.

6 Make a second earring.

Hanukkah earrings

1 Follow the chart using white thread and peyote stitch. Zip the ends together.

2 Attach a dark blue thread to the bead tube, exiting through one of the dark blue edge beads.

3 String three dark blue beads and pass through the next edge bead in the same direction to make a loop. Repeat around both edges of the earring.

4 On a head pin, string a 2.5 mm round gold bead, a blue cube bead, an 8 mm round gold bead, a bead tube, an 8 mm round gold bead, and a 2.5 mm round gold bead.

5 Make a plain loop at the top of the head pin. Attach to the ear wire.

6 Make a second earring.

Christmas earrings

1 Follow the chart using white thread and peyote stitch. Zip the ends together.

2 Attach a green thread to the bead tube, exiting through one of the green edge beads.

3 String three green beads and pass through the next edge bead in the same direction to make a loop. Repeat around both edges of the earring.

4 On a head pin, string a 4 mm gold round bead, an 8 mm gold round bead, a bead tube, and a 6 mm gold round bead.

5 Make a loop at the top of the head pin. Attach to the ear wire.

6 Make a second earring.

You'll need:

confetti earrings
- 11º cylinder beads
  - 3 g white
  - 1 g gold
  - 1 g red
  - 1 g glossy black
  - 1 g gray
- 2 2.5 mm round gold beads
- 2 8 mm round black beads
- white and gold beading thread

Hannukah earrings
- 11º cylinder beads, 1 g each:
  - light blue
  - white
  - blue
  - gold
- 4 2.5 mm round gold beads
- 2 3 mm cobalt blue cube beads
- white and dark blue beading thread

Christmas earrings
- 11º cylinder beads, 1 g each:
  - green
  - white
  - red
  - gold
- 2 4 mm round gold beads
- 2 6 mm round gold beads
- white and green beading thread

each project
- 8 mm round gold beads
- 2 3-in. (7.6 cm) gold head pins
- pair of gold ear wires
- scissors
- needle
- chainnose pliers
- roundnose pliers
- wire cutters

Topkapi Necklace

Topkapi Palace in Istanbul is a treasure trove of floral and geometric tiles on the floors, walls, and ceilings, often in a palette of cobalt blue, turquoise, and white. The Turkish Ottomans felt anything could be improved with a lot of gold; nothing was too over-the-top for the them. This necklace is a bit more subtle, but still has plenty of rich tones and a glimmer of gold.

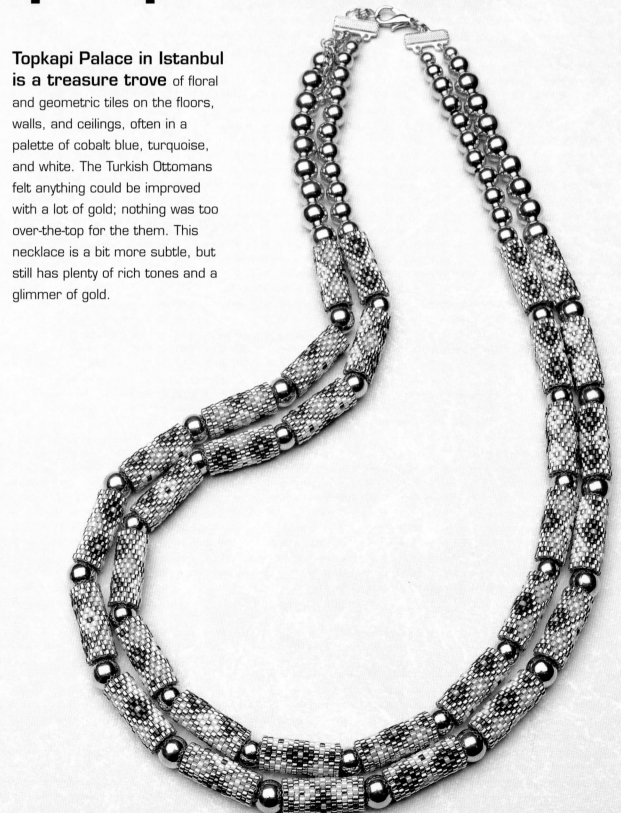

1 Following the chart and working in flat peyote stitch, make 32 beads, 16 with gold centers in the white diamonds and 16 with dark blue centers. (See arrows on the chart.) Fill each bead with a straw.

2 Cut two 28-in. (71 cm) lengths of beading wire.

TIP Use clamps on the ends of the beading wire to keep the strung beads from sliding off until you are ready to finish the ends.

3 On one strand of beading wire, string an 8 mm round gold bead and a bead tube alternately for a total of 16 times, ending with an 8 mm round gold bead for the outer strand of the necklace.

4 On the other strand of beading wire, string a 7 mm round gold bead and a bead tube alternately 16 times, ending with a 7 mm round gold bead for the inner strand. The differing round bead sizes will help the inner strand lie smoothly inside the outer strand.

5 On the outer strand of 8 mm round gold beads, string seven more 8 mm round gold beads, a 7 mm round gold bead, a 6 mm round gold bead and two crimp beads (for added strength). Pass the beading wire through one loop of the strand reducer and back through the crimp beads and gold beads. Crimp. Trim excess wire.

6 On the outer strand, on the other end of the beading wire, string seven more 8 mm round gold beads, a 7 mm round gold bead, a 6 mm round gold bead, and two crimp beads. Clamp so the beads won't fall off. Set aside.

7 On the inner strand of 7 mm round gold beads, string eight more 7 mm round gold beads, a 6 mm round gold bead, a 5 mm round gold bead, and two crimp beads. Pass through the other loop on the strand reducer and back through the crimp beads and gold beads. Crimp. Trim excess wire.

gold or dark blue

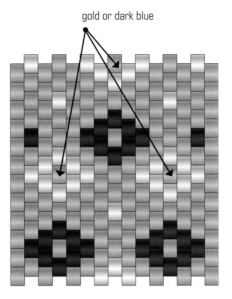

8 On the inner strand, on the other end of the beading wire, string eight more 7 mm round gold beads, a 6 mm round gold bead, a 5 mm round gold bead, and two crimp beads. Clamp so the beads won't fall off.

9 Before attaching the strung beads to the remaining strand reducer, make sure the strand reducers are facing upward and the two bead strands are lying smoothly. Adjust the slack in the beading wire, if necessary.

TIP If you lay the necklace flat and shape it into a circle, the bead tubes in each strand should be neatly paired. If you pick the necklace up, it will not look like they are lying in pairs.

10 Attach the bead strand to the strand reducer by removing the clamp, passing the beading wire through a loop on the reducer, and back through the crimp beads and gold beads. Crimp. Trim the excess wire. Repeat for the other bead strand.

11 Using the split rings, attach the lobster claw clasp to one strand reducer and the chain to the other reducer.

You'll need:

necklace, approximately 22 in. (56 cm), plus clasp

- 11° cylinder beads
  - 22 g gold
  - 7 g pearl
  - 7 g blue
  - 7 g light blue
- 31 8 mm round gold beads
- 35 7 mm round gold beads
- 2 6 mm round gold beads
- 4 5 mm round gold beads
- 2 gold strand reducers (2-to-1 connectors)
- 2 gold split rings
- 8 gold crimp beads
- gold beading wire, .019
- gold clasp, such as a lobster clasp and chain
- gold beading thread
- straws
- needle
- scissors
- chainnose or crimping pliers
- wire cutters

Tiny Venetians

This beautiful set feels old-world and ornate. Perhaps it's the slim beads that look like the mooring poles in front of the palazzi with their swirly barber-pole design. Maybe it's the crystals and pearls, which remind me of all the glass in Venice, the Pearl of the Adriatic. Either way, the combination is perfect for a delicate bracelet-and-earrings set.

bracelet

1 String 14 medium rose seed beads and work in flat peyote stitch for 12 rows (six on each side). Zip the ends together. Make two bead tubes.

2 String 14 pink ceylon seed beads and work in flat peyote stitch for 12 rows (six on each side). Zip the ends together.

3 String 14 dark cranberry seed beads and work in flat peyote stitch for 12 rows (six on each side). Zip the ends together.

4 Working in peyote stitch, follow the chart and make two patterned bead tubes.

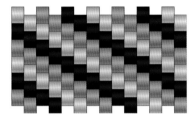

5 Cut 14 in. (36 cm) of beading wire. String a pearl, a 4 mm rose crystal, a 5 mm rose crystal, and two crimp beads. Slide the beads near the end of the beading wire. Go through a clasp loop and back through the crimp beads and a few more beads. Crimp. Trim excess wire.

6 String the bracelet: rose bead tube, pearl, 5 mm rose crystal, pearl bead, diagonal bead tube, pearl bead, 5 mm rose crystal, pearl bead, dark cranberry bead tube, pearl bead, 5 mm rose crystal, pearl bead, diagonal bead tube, pearl bead, 5 mm rose crystal, pearl, pink ceylon bead tube, pearl, 5 mm rose crystal, pearl, rose bead tube, pearl, 5 mm rose crystal, 4 mm rose crystal, two crimp beads, and the other half of clasp.

7 Pass the beading wire back through the crimp beads, crystals, and pearl. Pull snug. Crimp. Trim the excess wire.

earrings

1 Working in peyote stitch, follow the chart and make two bead tubes.

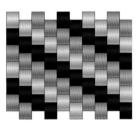

2 On the eye pin, string a bead tube and a 4 mm rose crystal. Make a plain loop and attach to the loop of the ear wire (or use the optional jump ring to attach to the ear wire).

3 On the head pin, string a 15º pink ceylon seed bead, a 3 mm light rose crystal, a 4 mm rose crystal, and a 2.5 mm pearl. Make a loop.

4 Attach to the eye pin bead assembly.

5 Repeat steps 2–4 for the other earring.

You'll need:

bracelet, approximately 8 in. (20 cm)
- 15º seed beads, 2 g each:
  - medium rose
  - pink ceylon
  - dark cranberry
- 7 5 mm rose bicone crystals
- 2 4 mm rose bicone crystals
- 12 4 mm pearls
- silver clasp
- 4 silver crimp beads
- beading wire, .019

earrings
- 15º seed beads, 1 g each:
  - medium rose
  - pink ceylon
  - dark cranberry
- 4 4 mm rose bicone crystals
- 2 3 mm light rose bicone crystals
- 2 2.5 mm pearls
- pair of silver ear wires
- 2 silver head pins
- 2 silver eye pins
- 2 small silver jump rings (optional)

both projects
- rose beading thread
- needle
- scissors
- chainnose pliers
- roundnose pliers
- wire cutters

Delhi Delight

Hot countries with intense sunlight demand equally intense colors. In India, you seldom see neutrals or pastels, only the brightest of colors. Diana Vreeland, legendary editor of *Vogue* magazine, once remarked that hot pink is the navy blue of India. Certainly when I visited, I saw plenty of hot pink—and red and yellow and turquoise—but the popular combination that year was lime green with cobalt blue. Take a chance, and make a statement in bold colors.

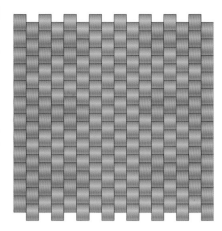

TIP This piece is made of many, many tubes in seven colors trimmed in gold. The tubes are strung with gold and filigree beads between them. This necklace is about 70 in. (1.78 m) long—you can make yours shorter or longer. Wear it long or looped around your neck several times.

necklace

1 Working in flat peyote stitch, follow the chart and make six bead tubes of each color cylinder bead, trimmed with the gold-lined crystal beads, for a total of 42 bead tubes. Fill each bead tube with straws or filler beads.

2 Cut a 76-in. (1.93 m) piece of beading wire. String two gold crimp beads, a 3 mm round gold bead, a 6 mm round gold bead, a 8 mm filigree bead, and a 6 mm round gold bead on the beading wire. Slide the beads near the end of the beading wire. Pass the end of the beading wire through a 12 mm gold ring and back through the crimp beads and all the gold beads. Crimp.

3 String the bead tubes, randomly selecting colors, with a 6 mm round gold bead, a 8 mm round filigree bead, and a 6 mm round gold bead between the bead tubes.

4 At the other end, string a 6 mm round gold bead, a 8 mm filigree bead, a 6 mm round gold bead, a 3 mm round gold bead, and two gold crimp beads. Pass the beading wire through a 12 mm gold ring and back through the crimp beads and all the gold beads. Leave a little slack in the necklace so it will curve nicely, but not so much that a lot of beading wire shows. Crimp. Trim the excess beading wire.

TASSELS

5 Thread a needle with about 5 ft. (1.52 m) of thread.

6 String seven gold-lined crystal beads. Tie into a circle with a square knot. Pass through the bead to the left of the knot.

7 String 36 beads of an opaque color, a 6 mm gold filigree bead, and a gold-lined crystal bead. Skipping the last bead, pass back through the filigree bead and an opaque color bead. String three opaque color beads, skip three beads, and pass through the next bead. Repeat to the top of the fringe strand. Pass through the bead on the ring in the same direction and into the next bead on the ring. Repeat for each opaque color for a total of seven fringes, one of each color. Bind off the thread ends in the top of the tassel.

8 On a gold head pin, string a 3 mm round gold bead, the tassel (insert the head pin through the center of the bead ring), a filigree bead cap, and a 3 mm round gold bead. Make a loop.

9 Repeat steps 5–8 to make a total of six tassels.

10 Open a 6 mm jump ring. String the 12 mm gold ring at one end of the necklace and the loop on one completed tassel. Close the jump ring. Repeat so the tassel is suspended from the gold ring by two jump rings. Repeat twice for a total of three tassels on the gold ring.

11 Repeat step 10 to make another triple tassel on the other end of the necklace.

You'll need:

lariat, approximately 70 in. (1.78 m)

- 18 g 11º cylinder beads, gold-lined crystal
- 11º cylinder beads, 5 g each
  - orange
  - yellow
  - turquoise
  - scarlet
  - purple
  - green
  - pink
- 14 3 mm round gold beads
- 86 6 mm round gold beads
- 42 6 mm round gold filigree beads
- 43 8 mm round gold filigree beads
- 6 gold filigree bead caps
- 12 6 mm gold jump rings
- 6 gold head pins
- 2 12 mm gold rings
- 4 gold crimp beads
- beading wire, .019
- straws or filler beads
- gold beading thread
- needle
- scissors
- chainnose pliers
- roundnose pliers
- wire cutters

You'll need:

3 bangles, approximately 3 in. (7.6 cm) diameter
- 9 g 11º cylinder beads, gold-lined crystal
- 11º cylinder beads, 3 g each:
  - orange
  - yellow
  - turquoise
  - scarlet
  - purple
  - green
  - rose pink
- 42 3 mm round gold beads
- 21 6 mm round gold filigree beads
- 6 gold crimp beads
- beading wire, .019

earrings
- 11º cylinder beads, 2 g each:
  - orange
  - yellow
  - turquoise
  - scarlet
  - purple
  - green
  - rose pink
- 28 11º cylinder beads, gold-lined crystal
- 2 gold filigree ear posts
- 2 gold filigree bead caps
- 14 6 mm round gold filigree beads
- 4 3 mm gold round beads
- 2 gold head pins
- 2 3 mm gold jump rings

all projects
- gold beading thread
- needle
- scissors
- chainnose pliers
- roundnose pliers
- wire cutters

bangles

TIP The bead tubes for the bangles are shorter than those for the necklace so they will better curve around your wrist. To make the bangles smaller or larger, adjust the number of bead tubes and spacer beads.

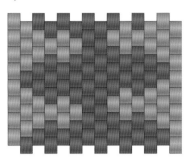

1 Working in flat peyote stitch, follow the chart to make one bead of each opaque color, trimmed with the gold-lined crystal beads. Fill each bead with straws.

2 Cut 15 in. (38 cm) of beading wire. String a bead tube, a 3 mm round gold bead, an 8 mm round filigree bead, and a 3 mm round gold bead. Repeat until you've strung all the bead tubes.

3 String two gold crimp beads. Pass the other end of the beading wire through the crimp beads so both beading wires pass through the crimp beads. Pull the wire snug. Crimp.

4 Pull the crimp beads inside one of the bead tubes. Trim the excess beading wire.

5 Repeat steps 1–4 to make two more bangles.

TIP To use a clasp, omit steps 3 and 4. Instead, attach the clasp at each end of the bracelet. Be sure to allow for the clasp in determining the length of your bracelet.

earrings

TIP The earrings are just one of the tassels from the necklace. If you don't mind the weight and want a more dramatic pair of earrings, make three tassels for each ear and slide them on to a large hoop earring.

1 Following steps 5–8 for the necklace, make two tassels.

2 Use a 3 mm gold jump ring to attach each tassel to the filigree ear post.

Christmas Charm Bracelet

For holiday parties, what could be better than a green-and-white bracelet with Christmas-themed charms and jingle bells? This quick-and-easy piece is perfect for last-minute gifts or get-togethers.

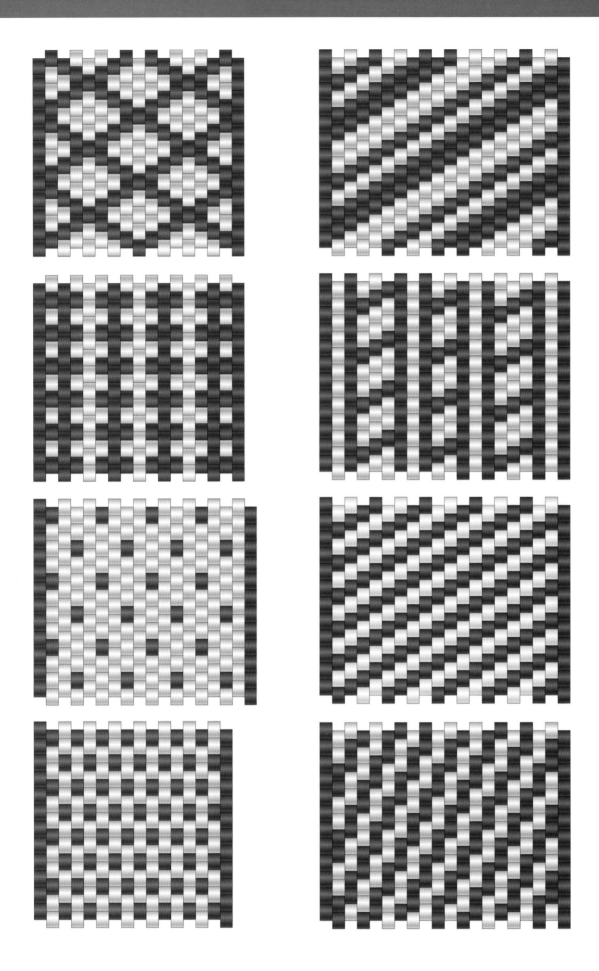

1 Working in flat peyote stitch, follow the charts and make one bead in each pattern using your choice of green and white beads. Fill each bead with a straw.

2 On a head pin, string a 7 mm round silver bead or jingle bell, a bead tube, a 7 mm round silver bead, and a 3 mm round silver bead. Make a loop. Repeat for all the bead tubes.

3 Attach the bead tubes and charms, one at a time, to each link on the bracelet using jump ring. Attach the remaining charm to the clasp.

TIP My bracelet chain was 9 in. (23 cm) long. I started adding the charms and bead tubes near the lobster clasp end of the chain so I could clip through any of the remaining links at the other end and let the snowflake charm dangle.

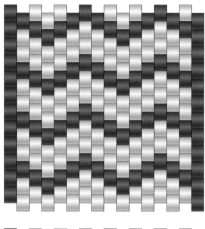

You'll need:

bracelet, approximately 8 in. (20 cm)
- 11° cylinder beads
  - 7 g medium green and dark green mixture
  - 7 g white
- 10 Christmas charms in silver, red, green, and white
- 10 3 mm round silver beads
- 20 7 mm round silver beads or 10 7 mm round silver beads and 10 silver jingle bells
- 7–9 in. (18–23 cm) bracelet, medium link, silver, with clasp
- 20 6 mm silver jump rings
- 10 silver head pins
- white beading thread
- straws
- scissors
- needle
- chainnose pliers
- roundnose pliers
- wire cutters

Chinese Coin Charm Earrings

Even if you haven't explored the Far East yet, Chinatown, whether in New York or San Francisco, always seems to have festive red-and-gold Chinese lanterns bobbing in the breeze. Chinese coin charms are easy to find at bead shops. Make a colorful lantern-like design to showcase your coin charms and remind you of a great vacation—or let the jewelry inspire you to visit someday.

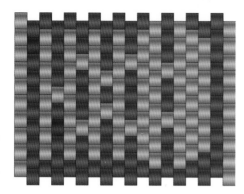

Happiness Ideogram

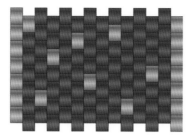

Random Dots

You'll need:

- 11º cylinder beads
  - 4 g mixed red
  - 2 g gold
- 2 gold Chinese coin charms
- pair of gold earring posts
- 2 gold eye pins
- 4 4 mm round gold beads
- jump rings, optional
- E6000 adhesive
- red beading thread
- needle
- scissors
- chainnose pliers
- roundnose pliers
- wire cutters

1 Using flat peyote stitch, work the Happiness Ideogram. Zip the ends together. Make two. Insert straws in the bead tubes.

2 Using flat peyote stitch, work the Random Dots chart. Zip the ends together. Make four.

3 Glue a small Random Dots bead tube to each side of the larger Happiness Ideogram bead tube with a small line of glue, centering the smaller tubes on each side of the larger tube. Repeat with the remaining tubes. Let dry thoroughly.

4 Attach the coin charm to the loop of an eye pin.

5 On the eye pin, string a 4 mm gold bead, an assembled bead units through the center bead tube, and a 4 mm gold bead. Make a plain loop. Attach the eye pin to the earring post.

6 Repeat steps 4–5 to make a second earring.

TIP Work on waxed paper when gluing. Glue does not stick well to waxed paper, and your jewelry won't either. Plus it's easy to clean up—just wad the paper up and throw it away.

Bronze Columns

The simplest of designs can create some extremely sophisticated jewelry. I began with some unusual bead shapes—triangles and hexes—in an interesting color: iridescent bronze. A macramé cord adds yet another dimension of interest with more texture.

necklace

1 Make a ladder of 12 twisted hex beads. Join the ends to make a circle.

2 Working in tubular brick stitch, alternate rows of triangle and hex beads for 23 rows, ending with a row of twisted hex beads. Insert the straw, if desired.

3 On a head pin, string a brown metal bead, barrel bead, brown metal bead, bead tube, and brown metal bead. Make a plain loop.

4 Slide the completed bead tube on the pendant strands of the macramé neck cord, weaving through the head pin loop and tying a square knot securely between the loop and bead. Use a needle to pull the remaining cord into the bead tube. Trim any excess cord at the bottom of the bead tube.

bracelet

1 Make a ladder of 12 twisted hex beads. Join the ends to make a circle.

2 Work in tubular brick stitch for nine rows using twisted hex beads. Insert a straw.

3 Repeat steps 1 and 2 to make a second bead.

4 For the third bead, make a ladder of 12 twisted hex beads. Join the ends to make a circle. Then work in tubular brick stitch, alternating rows of triangle and hex beads for eight rows, ending with a twisted hex bead row. Insert a straw.

5 Cut a 14-in. (36 cm) piece of beading wire. String an 8 mm brown metal bead, two or more 4 mm beads, and a crimp bead. Go through the loop on the clasp, the crimp bead, and a few more beads. Pull snug. Crimp.

TIP Use additional 4 mm metal beads to adjust the length of the bracelet.

6 String: barrel bead, 8 mm brown metal bead, bead tube from steps 1 and 2, 8 mm brown metal bead, barrel bead, 8 mm brown metal bead, bead tube from step 3, 8 mm brown metal bead, barrel bead, 8 mm brown metal bead, bead tube from steps 1 and 2, 8 mm brown metal bead, barrel bead, 8 mm brown metal bead, two or more 4 mm beads, crimp bead. Go through the loop on the clasp, the crimp bead, and a few more beads. Pull snug. Crimp. Trim excess wire.

earrings

1 String a hex bead and a triangle bead. Repeat twice for a total of six beads.

2 Using flat peyote stitch, bead 18 rows (nine on each side), matching the new beads in each row to the bead immediately below them to create stripes of hex and triangle beads. Add rows to fit around your hoop earrings as necessary.

3 Fold the peyote strip around the hoop earring and zip the ends together.

4 Make a second earring.

TIP Finding a bronze-colored hoop earring can be difficult. Look through discount stores, flea markets, and tourist shops as well as bead shops and bead shows. You never know where a good bead or a good finding is hiding!

You'll need:

necklace, approximately 18 in. (46 cm) with 4 in. (10 cm) pendant
- 5 g 11º matte bronze triangle beads
- 5 g 11º bronze twisted hex beads
- 12 x 9 mm barrel bead, bronze iridescent finish
- 3 8 mm brown metal beads
- 18 in. (46 cm) brown macramé neck cord with strands for pendant
- straw (optional)
- 5 in. (13 cm) gold head pin
- chainnose pliers
- roundnose pliers
- wire cutters

bracelet, 8 in. (20 cm)
- 2 g 11º matte bronze triangle beads
- 5 g 11º bronze twisted hex beads
- 4 12 x 9 mm barrel beads, bronze iridescent finish
- 8 8 mm brown metal beads
- 4 or more 4 mm bronze metal beads
- beading wire, .019
- 2 crimp beads
- bronze or copper clasp
- straw
- chainnose or crimping pliers
- wire cutters

earrings
- 1 g 11º matte bronze triangle beads
- 1 g 11º bronze twisted hex beads
- bronze hoop earrings, approximately 1 in. (2.5 cm) diameter

all projects
- brown beading thread
- needle
- scissors

Copper and Silver Set

I bought these copper-and-silver beads years ago in a funky hippie kind of shop. Bead tubes were the answer for showing them off! A few simple designs in a dramatic color scheme tied one bead to another, making a great bracelet. The earrings are simply two more of the copper-and-silver beads.

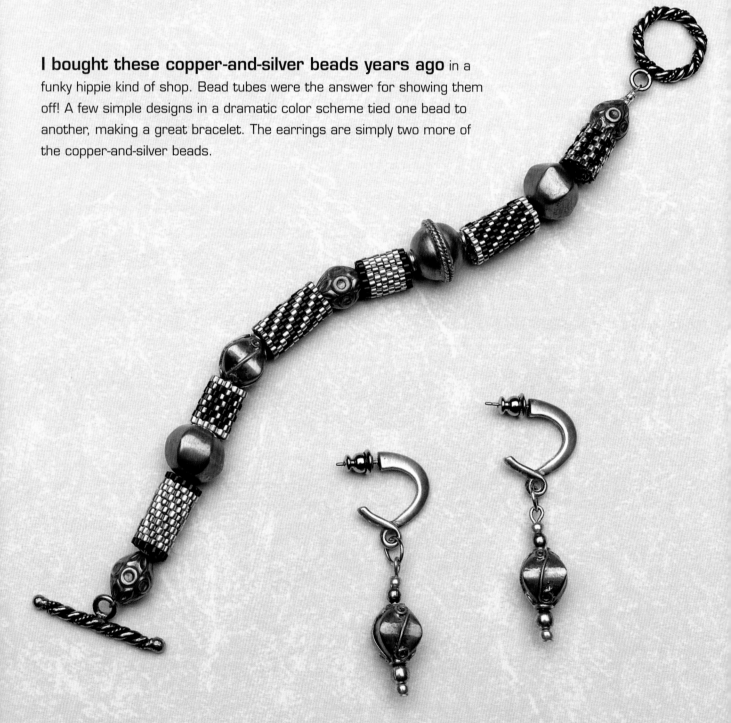

TIP Do you have some wonderful orphan beads you haven't been able to make into something fabulous to wear? Try combining them with bead tubes and see what happens!

bracelet

1 Use each chart to make three beads, varying the color positions, for a total of six beads. Fill with straws or use filler beads when assembling the bracelet.

2 Cut 12 in. (30 cm) of beading wire. String one copper-and-silver bead and one bead tube. Alternate copper-and-silver beads and bead tubes to the end of the bracelet, ending with a copper-and-silver bead. Check the fit, and add or remove beads as necessary.

3 String two crimp beads, and go through half of the clasp and back through the crimp beads. Pull snug. Crimp and trim the excess wire. Repeat on the other end of the bracelet with the other half of the clasp.

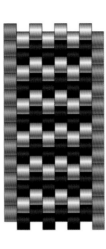

earrings

1 On a head pin, string: 3 mm silver bead, 4 mm silver bead, copper-and-silver bead, 4 mm silver bead, 3 mm silver bead. Make a loop.

2 Attach the component to an earring finding with a jump ring.

3 Make a second earring.

TIP If you don't have enough copper-and-silver beads to make the earrings, why not make a couple of matching bead tubes and assemble them into earrings?

Materials

bracelet, approximately 6½ in. (16.5 cm)
- 11º cylinder beads, 2 g each:
  - galvanized silver
  - copper
  - glossy black
- 7 copper-and-silver beads
- copper toggle clasp
- 4 silver or copper crimp beads
- beading wire, .019
- beading thread
- straws or filler beads
- needle
- scissors
- chainnose or crimping pliers

earrings
- 2 copper-and-silver beads
- 4 4 mm silver beads
- 4 3 mm silver beads
- 2 silver head pins
- 2 jump rings
- pair of silver ear posts
- roundnose pliers

both projects
- chainnose pliers
- wire cutters

Paramount Theater Set

Before multiplexes, movie theaters were
often imaginatively decorated. The exteriors were always
as lavishly decorated with as much neon as the owner could
afford. These banded bead tubes remind me of some of
those blinking, moving, layered fantasy worlds that I visited on
Saturday afternoons for the double matinee, which included
one or more cartoons and the newsreel of the week. It was
the world of popcorn, jujubes, soda pop, and movie stars.

necklace

LARGE BANDED BEAD TUBE

1 For the inner core, string a gold bead, 20 purple beads, and a gold bead.

2 Work in peyote stitch for a total of 20 rows (10 on each side). Zip the ends together.

3 For the second layer of beads, string a gold bead, 10 pink beads, and a gold bead.

4 Work in peyote stitch for a total of 32 rows (16 on each side).

5 Wrap the bead band around the center of the purple inner core and zip the ends together.

6 For the top layer, string a gold bead, four turquoise beads, and a gold bead.

7 Work in peyote stitch for a total of 44 rows (22 on each side).

8 Wrap the bead band around the center of the second layer and zip the ends together.

SMALL BANDED BEAD TUBES

9 For the inner core, make a ladder four gold beads long. Join the ends to make a circle.

10 Using purple beads, work in tubular brick stitch for 16 rows.

11 Work one row of gold beads to finish.

12 For the second layer, string a gold bead, eight pink beads, and a gold bead.

13 Work in peyote stitch for a total of 20 rows (10 on each side).

14 Wrap the bead band around the purple inner core and zip the ends together.

15 For the top layer, string a gold bead, two turquoise beads, and a gold bead.

16 Work in peyote stitch for a total of 30 rows (15 on each side).

17 Wrap the bead band around the center of the second layer and zip the ends together.

18 Repeat steps 9–17 to make three more beads.

PLAIN TUBE BEADS

19 String a gold bead, 14 colored beads, and a gold bead.

20 Work in peyote stitch for a total of 20 rows (10 on each side). Zip the ends together.

21 Repeat steps 19 and 20 until you have four plain beads of each color.

ASSEMBLE THE NECKLACE

22 Cut 28 in. (71 cm) of gold beading wire, and string two crimp beads, a 3 mm round gold bead, a 6 mm round gold bead, a 7 mm round gold bead, and an 8 mm round gold bead. Slide the beads near the end of the beading wire. Pass the end of the beading wire through a split ring and back through the crimp beads and all the gold beads. Crimp. Trim the excess wire.

23 String the beads on the beading wire:

purple tube bead	→ 8 mm gold bead
pink tube bead	→ 8 mm gold bead
turquoise tube bead	→ 8 mm gold bead
purple tube bead	→ 8 mm gold bead
small banded tube bead	→ 8 mm gold bead
pink tube bead	→ 8 mm gold bead
small tube banded bead	→ 8 mm gold bead
turquoise tube bead	→ 8 mm gold bead
large banded tube bead	→ 8 mm gold bead
turquoise tube bead	→ 8 mm gold bead
small banded tube bead	→ 8 mm gold bead
pink tube bead	→ 8 mm gold bead
small banded tube bead	→ 8 mm gold bead
purple tube bead	→ 8 mm gold bead
turquoise tube bead	→ 8 mm gold bead
pink tube bead	→ 8 mm gold bead
purple tube bead	

24 At the end of the tube beads, string an 8 mm round gold bead, a 7 mm round gold bead, a 6 mm round gold bead, a 3 mm round gold bead, two gold crimp beads, and a split ring. Pass back through the crimp beads and round gold beads. Crimp. Trim the excess wire.

25 Using the jump rings, attach the clasp to the split rings on each end of the necklace.

You'll need:

necklace, 22 in. (58 cm) long
- 11º cylinder beads, 10 g each:
  - purple
  - rose pink
  - turquoise
- 5 g 11º cylinder beads, gold-lined crystal
- 18 8 mm round gold beads
- 2 7 mm round gold beads
- 2 6 mm round gold beads
- 2 3 mm round gold beads
- gold clasp
- 2 6 mm gold split rings
- 4 gold crimp beads
- 2 4 mm gold jump rings
- gold beading wire, .019

earrings
- 11º cylinder beads, 2 g each:
  - purple
  - rose pink
  - turquoise
- 1 g 11º cylinder beads, gold-lined crystal
- 2 8 mm round gold beads
- 2 3 mm round gold beads
- 2 2-in. (5 cm) gold head pins
- 2 2-in. gold eye pins
- 2 4–6 mm gold jump rings
- pair of half-dome gold ear posts with loop

both projects
- gold beading thread
- needle
- scissors
- chainnose or crimping pliers
- wire cutters

earrings

1 For the inner core, make a bead ladder four gold beads long. Join the ends to make a ring.

2 Using purple beads, work in tubular brick stitch for 28 rows.

3 Stitch one row of gold beads to finish.

4 For the second layer, string a gold bead, 16 pink beads, and a gold bead.

5 Work in peyote stitch for a total of 20 rows (10 on each side).

6 Wrap the band around the inner core and zip the ends together.

7 For the top layer, string a gold bead, six turquoise beads, and a gold bead.

8 Work in peyote stitch for a total of 32 rows (16 on each side).

9 Wrap the band around the second layer and zip the ends together.

10 Repeat steps 1–9 to make a second bead.

11 On a short gold head pin, string a 3mm round gold bead and an 8mm round gold bead. Make a loop.

12 Insert an eye pin through the purple inner core of a layered bead. Make a loop at the top.

13 Attach the head pin dangle to the eye loop at the bottom of the layered bead.

14 Use a small jump ring to attach the layered bead assembly to the ear post loop.

15 Repeat steps 11–14 to make a second earring.

Tibetan Fantasy

Tibetan jewelry often has old, heavily worked silver, turquoise stones, and cinnabar accents. The cinnabar is a beautiful orangey-red that accepts both turquoise and silver perfectly. While you make this piece, you can imagine trekking the Himalayas, visiting the villages, and looking at beautiful textiles and jewelry.

necklace

1 Leave a long tail of Fireline, and string a gray bead, two 15º red beads, four gray beads, two turquoise beads, and two gray beads. Tie into a circle.

2 Pass through the first bead strung. Start peyote by stringing the color bead you are exiting, skipping a bead, and going through a bead. Continue around the circle, working in odd-count tubular peyote. Make sure your first rows don't twist. Continue stringing the color bead you are exiting. The colors will form a spiral. Make the tube 20 in. (51 cm) long. After the first inch or two, work around the rattail cord.

3 At the end, secure the rattail cord inside each end of the tube with stitches through the cord and the beads of the tube. Trim the excess rattail cord.

4 Finish the end of the tube by decreasing every other bead until only two are left. To decrease, instead of stringing a new bead to make the next stitch, leave the space empty and pass through the next bead. Secure with a couple of knots. Leave the remaining Fireline to use later to attach the clasp.

5 Thread the tail thread at the other end on your needle and repeat step 4.

PENDANT

6 Using gray beading thread, string a turquoise bead, a 15º red bead, 30 gray beads, a 15º red bead, and a turquoise bead. Work 16 rows of flat peyote stitch (eight beads on each side). Zip the ends together. Make five beads.

7 String a turquoise bead, a 15º red bead, 18 gray beads, a 15º red bead, and a turquoise bead. Work 16 rows of peyote stitch (eight beads on each side). Zip the ends together. Make two beads.

8 String a turquoise bead, a 15º red bead, six gray beads, a 15º red bead, and a turquoise bead. Work 16 rows of peyote stitch (eight beads on each side). Zip the ends together.

9 String a turquoise bead, a 15º red bead, six gray beads, one 15º red bead, and a turquoise bead. Work 30 rows of peyote stitch (15 beads on each side). This bead tube will slide onto the tubular necklace, so be sure it fits around the necklace tube before zipping the ends together.

10 Insert straws into each of the pendant bead tubes. Position the five long bead tubes side by side, with the medium and small tubes at the bottom, and the other medium tube and large tube on top. Glue the pendant bead tubes together, centering each bead tube over the previous bead tube. Let dry throughly.

TIP You may want to glue only one or two pendant bead tubes together at one time, letting each dry throughly before adding another bead tube. Work on wax paper so that the partially assembled pendant does not stick to the working surface.

11 Glue the cinnabar charm to the assembled pendant. Let dry throughly.

12 Slide the top bead tube of the pendant over the necklace tube.

13 Using the Fireline left on each end of the necklace tube, attach the split rings for the clasp by sewing through a split ring and the last two beads several times. Attach the clasp with jump rings.

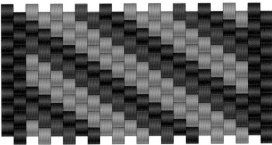

earrings

1 Working in flat peyote stitch, follow the chart. Zip the ends together to make two bead tubes.

2 String a red bead, 14 gray beads, and a red bead. Work in flat peyote stitch for 16 rows (eight beads on each side). Zip the ends together. Make four bead tubes.

3 Glue a small bead tube to each side of a large bead tube, centering the smaller tubes on each side of the larger tube. Repeat for the other earring. Let dry thoroughly.

4 On a decorative head pin, string a red seed bead, a rectangular decorative bead, an assembled bead tube unit, a round silver bead, and a red seed bead. Make a loop. Attach to an ear wire loop.

5 Repeat for the other earring.

TIP When the glue is dry, you can use pointed tweezers and toothpicks to remove any excess glue. Very judicious use of nail polish remover on cotton swab sticks can also be helpful to remove excess glue. But be careful not to remove the finish on your beads!

You'll need:

necklace, approximately 22 in. (56 cm) plus pendant
- 11º seed beads
  - 10 g turquoise
  - 40 g olive gray
- 5 g 15º seed beads, dark red
- decorative cinnabar pendant or flat bead
- 2 small silver split rings
- 2 small jump rings
- silver clasp
- Fireline 6-lb. test, smoke
- rattail cord, approximately 24 in. (61 cm)
- straws

earrings
- 15º seed beads
  - 2 g dark red
  - 2 g turquoise
  - 5 g olive gray
- 2 decorative silver head pins
- 2 silver rectangular beads
- 2 6–8 mm round silver beads
- pair of silver ear wires

both projects
- gray beading thread
- E6000 adhesive
- needle
- scissors
- chainnose pliers
- roundnose pliers
- wire cutters

Chakra Pop-Top Charm Bracelet

Charm bracelets were especially popular in the 1950s and 1960s. Many women had several with mementos from trips or special occasions. For a twist on tradition, combine new-age philosophy with found or recycled materials in this eclectic piece.

Designed and beaded by Linda McGill

1 Following the charts, work in flat peyote stitch to make one bead tube in each color from each chart (14 total beads, seven of each size).

TIP Vary the placement of the black cylinder beads on each bead tube, if you like, for a random pattern.

2 On a head pin, string an 11º black cylinder bead, a 3 mm black bead, a 5 mm black bead, a bead tube, filler beads to fill the bead tube, a 5 mm black bead, a 3 mm black bead, and an 11º black cylinder bead. Make a loop. Repeat for each bead tube.

3 On a head pin, string an 11º black cylinder bead, a crystal, and an 11º black cylinder bead. Make a loop. Repeat for each crystal.

4 On a head pin, string an 11º black cylinder bead, a 3 mm black bead, a bottle cap bead, a 3 mm black bead, and an 11º black cylinder bead. Make a loop. Repeat for each bottle cap bead.

5 Attach on half of the clasp to each end of the chain.

6 About 1 in. (2.5 cm) from an end, in a bracelet chain link, string one jump ring with a large red bead tube and a matching red bottle cap bead. Close the jump ring. In the same link, attach a smaller red bead tube and a matching red crystal with a jump ring.

7 Repeat for the rest of the bead tubes, bottle cap beads, and crystals in this order: orange, yellow, green, turquoise, blue, and violet. This is the chakra color sequence. Wear it in good health and with good vibrations!

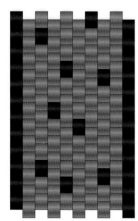

large chakra

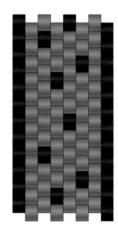

small chakra

You'll need:

bracelet, approximately 7 in. (18 cm)
- 11º cylinder beads, 3 g each:
  - matte violet
  - matte dark aqua
  - matte turquoise
  - matte dark jade
  - matte yellow
  - matte orange
  - matte dark red
- 4 g 11º cylinder beads, matte black
- 7 bottle-cap charms in colors similar to beads
- 7 8 mm crystals or Czech glass beads in colors similar to beads
- 6–7 in. (15–18 cm) dark pewter or black chain
- dark pewter or black clasp
- 14 dark pewter or black jump rings
- 28 3-in. (7.6 cm) dark pewter or black head pins
- 28 5 mm black beads
- 42 3 mm black beads
- 2–3 g 8º black filler beads
- black beading thread
- needle
- scissors
- chainnose pliers
- roundnose pliers
- wire cutters

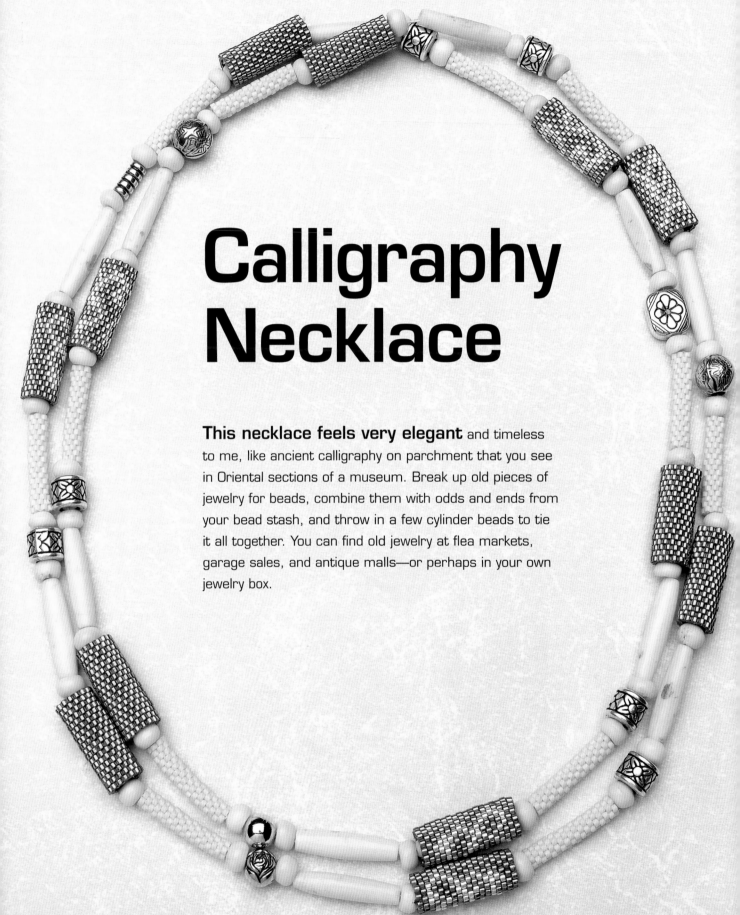

Calligraphy Necklace

This necklace feels very elegant and timeless to me, like ancient calligraphy on parchment that you see in Oriental sections of a museum. Break up old pieces of jewelry for beads, combine them with odds and ends from your bead stash, and throw in a few cylinder beads to tie it all together. You can find old jewelry at flea markets, garage sales, and antique malls—or perhaps in your own jewelry box.

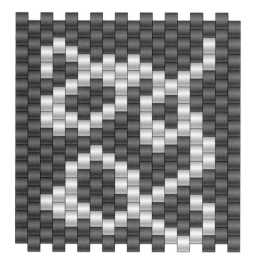

TIP To protect the finish on metallic beads, soak them in clear acrylic floor finish before assembling the necklace.

You'll need:

necklace, 48 in. (1.22 m)

- 11º cylinder beads
  - 20 g dark gold
  - 10 g dark cream matte
  - 3 g galvanized silver
- 12 5 x 24 mm oval ivory-colored bone or plastic tubes
- 48 5 x 7 mm round ivory-colored bone or plastic beads
- 12 miscellaneous design silver beads
- silver crimp bead
- silver clasp (optional)
- 4 g 8º filler beads for gold and calligraphy cylinder beads
- white and gold beading thread
- beading wire, .019
- needle
- scissors
- chainnose or crimping pliers
- wire cutters

PLAIN GOLD BEAD TUBE

1 String 18 gold beads. Work in flat peyote stitch for a total of 28 rows (14 beads on each side). Zip the ends together. Make six beads.

PLAIN CREAM BEAD TUBE

2 String 18 dark cream matte beads. Work in flat peyote stitch for a total of 12 rows (six on each side). Zip the ends together. Make 12 beads.

CALLIGRAPHY BEAD TUBE

3 Following the chart, work in flat peyote stitch, using dark gold and galvanized silver beads, and zip the ends together. Make six beads.

4 Cut 52 in. (1.32 m) of beading wire. String: round bone bead, oval bone bead, round bone bead, silver bead, round bone bead, cream bead tube from step 2, round bone bead, gold bead tube from step 1, round bone bead, oval bone bead, round bone bead, silver bead, round bone bead, ivory bead tube, round bone bead, calligraphy bead tube from step 3. (Fill each bead tube with filler beads as you string the necklace.) Repeat five times.

TIP If your silver beads have large-diameter holes, use small filler beads to keep them centered.

5 Attach a clasp on each end, or make a continuous necklace: Pull both ends of the beading wire through two or more crimp beads in opposite directions. Pull the wire snug, leaving a little slack, and crimp. Trim the excess wire. Hide the crimped beading wire section inside a bead tube.

TIP To prevent beads from sliding off while you are stringing the necklace, put a clamp or a large stop bead on the end of the beading wire.

Whirligig Necklace

Make the Whirligig Necklace in pop psychedelic colors, whirling off in all directions. Hot pink and lime green are youthful and cheerful—so stitch up a fun bubblegum necklace for you or your favorite teenybopper.

FRINGED BEAD

1 String five white, six pink, four white, and six green seed beads. Tie into a circle. This bead tube should be approximately ½ in. (1.3 cm) in diameter.

2 Pass through the first bead strung. Start peyote stitch by stringing the color bead your thread is exiting, skipping a bead, and going through a bead. Continue around the circle, working in odd-count tubular peyote. Continue stringing the color bead you are exiting. Make the tube about 1¼ in. (3.2 cm) long.

3 Fringes are worked from each bead of the tube. Pass through a bead on a bead tube. Matching the fringed bead color to the color of the tube, string 6–10 beads. Skipping the last bead strung, pass back through all the beads in the fringe and through the bead on the tube again in the same direction. Pass through another bead on the tube and repeat until all beads on the bead tube have a fringe. You may want to vary the fringe systematically, such as 6–8–10–8–6 or 6–8 on one row and 8–10 on the next.

TIP Make a half-hitch knot occasionally. If one of the fringes breaks, only a few fringes will come undone.

NECKLACE TUBE

4 String one white, four pink, two white, and four green seed beads. Tie into a circle. This tube should be about about ⅜ in. (1 cm) in diameter. The fringed bead should slip over it easily.

5 Follow the directions in step 2 for working odd-count tubular peyote. When the tube is about 1-in. (2.5 cm) long, slide it onto the rattail cord. Continue working the tube around the rattail cord until the tube is about 24 in. (61 cm) long.

6 At the end, secure the rattail cord inside each end of the tube with a few stitches through the rattail cord and the bead tube. Trim the excess cord.

7 Decrease the end of the tube, following the color pattern, until two beads remain: To decrease, do not string a bead; just pass through the next up-bead and pull together snugly.

8 Add one half of the clasp by stitching through the clasp ring and two remaining beads several times.

TIP To prevent fraying, I often coat the threads attaching a clasp with clear nail polish or glue.

9 Slide the fringed bead on the necklace tube.

10 Repeat steps 6–8.

You'll need:

necklace, 24 in. (61 cm) plus clasp

- 11º seed beads, approximately 25 g each:
    - white
    - neon pink
    - neon green
- white beading thread
- rattail or other cord, about 30 in. (76 cm) long
- clasp
- needle
- scissors

Starry Night

This bracelet reminds me of mild summer nights with millions of stars shining overhead. Maybe it reminds you of crisp, cold winter nights with the Milky Way sprawling overhead. Try a midnight blue or deep, deep purple instead of black to commemorate one of those memories.

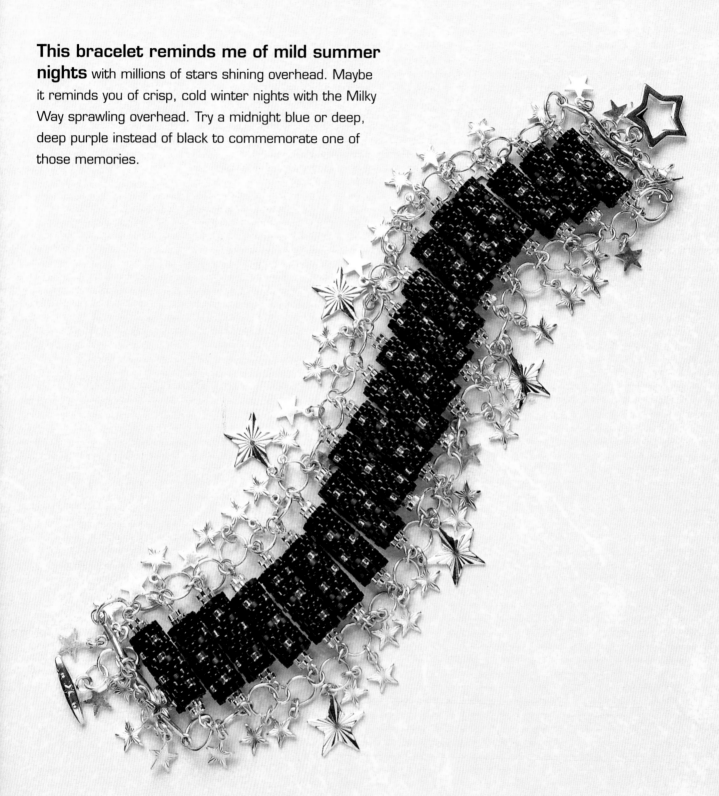

bracelet

1 Using white thread, make a ladder of silver-lined crystal beads four beads long. Join the ends to make a circle.

2 Work in tubular brick stitch for another 17 rows. Make 20 beads.

3 Using black thread, string 14 mixed black beads. Work in flat peyote stitch for 20 total rows (10 beads on each side), inserting silver-lined crystal beads randomly.

4 Wrap the flat black peyote piece around a silver-lined crystal core bead from steps 1 and 2, Zip the ends together.

5 Push an eye pin through the center of the silver-lined crystal core bead lengthwise. Make a loop the same size as the eye pin loop. Use your pliers to straighten the loops on each end of the pin so they are facing the same direction. Make 20 beads.

6 Attach a 4 mm jump ring to the eye pin loops at each end of each bead.

7 Using a 6 mm jump ring, connect the 4 mm ring from the ends of two bead tubes. Connect the two 4 mm jump rings on the other ends with another 6 mm jump ring. Continue adding one bead tube at a time, checking that the rings and beads are not twisted so that they will lie flat when all 20 bead tubes are connected.

TIP If you keep the loops of the pins in the beads horizontal so the 4 mm jump rings are vertical, the 6 mm jump rings will also lie horizontally.

8 Use 8 mm jump rings to connect the loops of the bars to the last bead tube on each end.

9 Attach half of the clasp to each bracelet bar with jump rings.

10 Use 4 mm jump rings to add one or more 6 mm or 10 mm stars to each 6 mm jump ring in the bracelet. Use jump rings to attach stars to the loops on the bracelet bars.

TIP Open and close the jump rings carefully so they close tightly. You can also put the tiniest dab of G-S Hypo Cement on the opening of each jump ring to seal it shut after you close it. I seal them all at once before I add the stars, but you may find it easier to seal them one at a time as you go.

TIP It can be difficult to bead randomly. Our minds always want to create a pattern, or we may put in too few or too many accent beads. Here's a trick you can use: Decide how many random accent beads you want, perhaps 4–5% of the total. Use a deck of 52 playing cards. For each bead you add, turn over one card. Whenever a red queen appears, insert an accent bead. When you finish the deck, shuffle and start over. As there are two red queens in the deck, you'll have about 4% accent beads.

You'll need:

bracelet, approximately 8 in. (20 cm)
- 11º cylinder beads
    - 20 g glossy and matte black
    - 15 g silver-lined crystal
- 120 4 mm silver jump rings
- 50 6 mm silver jump rings
- 4 8 mm silver jump rings
- 20 silver eye pins
- 60 6 mm silver stars
- 10 10 mm silver stars
- silver star toggle clasp
- twig earring finding or 25 mm 2-to-1 connector

necklace, approximately 24 in. (61 cm) plus pendant
- 11º cylinder beads
    - 6 g glossy and matte black
    - 1 g silver-lined crystal
- 9 4 mm silver jump rings
- 6 mm silver jump ring
- silver eye pin
- 2 silver head pins
- 6 6 mm silver stars
- 3 10 mm silver stars
- 24 in. (61 cm) silver snake-chain necklace
- 3 6 mm glossy black beads
- E6000 adhesive

earrings
- 11º cylinder beads
    - 3 g glossy and matte black
    - 2 g silver-lined crystal
- 6 4 mm silver jump rings
- 2 silver eye pins
- 4 6 mm silver stars
- 2 10 mm silver stars
- pair of silver ear wires

all projects
- white and black beading thread
- needle
- scissors
- chainnose pliers
- roundnose pliers
- wire cutters

necklace

1 String 20 mixed black beads. Work in flat peyote stitch for 12 rows (6 beads on each side), inserting silver-lined crystal beads randomly. Zip the ends together.

2 String 26 mixed black beads. Work in flat peyote stitch for 12 rows (6 beads on each side), inserting silver-lined crystal beads randomly. Zip the ends together.

3 String 34 mixed black beads. Work in flat peyote stitch for 12 rows (17 on each side), inserting silver-lined crystal beads randomly. Zip the ends together.

4 Insert a straw into each bead tube.

5 On a head pin, string a round black bead and the bead tube from step 1. Make a loop. Attach two 6 mm stars and a 10 mm star using 4 mm jump rings.

6 Repeat for the bead tube from step 2.

7 On the eye pin, string a round black bead and the bead tube from step 3. Make a loop. Attach two 6 mm stars and a 10 mm star using 4 mm jump rings. Attach the 7 mm jump ring to the eye pin loop on the opposite end.

8 Glue the assembled bead tubes together, placing the shorter bead tubes on each side of the larger one, slightly to the rear of the center bead, to form an arch rather than a flat pendant.

9 When thoroughly dry, slide the bead tube pendant on the necklace chain.

earrings

1 Following steps 1–5 of the bracelet instructions, make two beads.

2 Using 4 mm jump rings, attach a 10 mm and two 6 mm stars to the bottom loop of a bead tube.

3 Attach the top loop of the bead tube to the ear wire.

4 Repeat steps 2–3 to make a second earring.

Safari Set

I've always wanted to go on safari with tents and native dancers, lions, elephants, and zebras. I admire African beads in colors that seem so old and powerful and dusty. These pieces are a tribute to the trip I'd like to take someday.

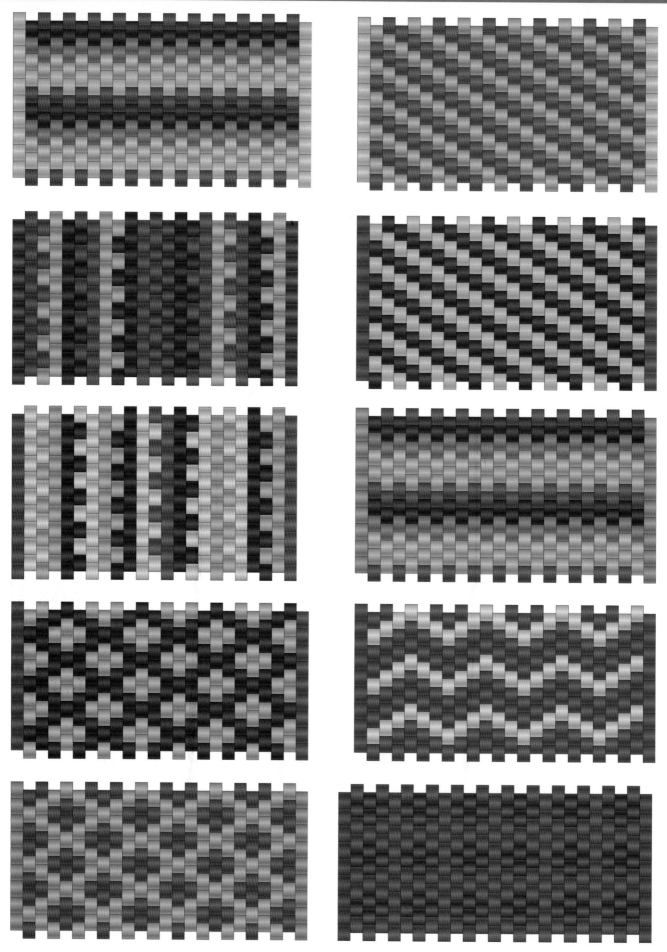

TIP Bison and armadillos may not shout "Africa" to you, but they were in the animal bead set I bought. You might be able to find animals that are more representative for your piece.

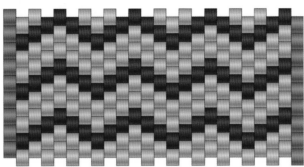

necklace

1 Working in flat peyote stitch, make one bead tube from each chart for a total of 12 bead tubes. Fill each tube with a straw.

2 Cut a 1-yd. (.9 m) piece of beading wire. String a crimp bead and a 3 mm round gold bead. Slide the beads near the end of the beading wire. Pass the short tail through a split ring and back through the crimp bead and 3 mm bead. Crimp.

3 String four 7 mm round wooden beads. Then alternate oval and round wooden beads for a total of 23 sets. String three round wooden beads, a 3 mm gold bead, a crimp bead, and a split ring. Go back through the crimp bead, gold bead, and a few wooden beads. Crimp. Trim the excess beading wire.

4 Thread the needle with Fireline. Pass the needle through two or three of the wooden beads at one end of the necklace. Pull most of the Fireline through the beads. Tie a half-hitch knot around the beading wire between the wooden beads of the necklace. Repeat two or three more times, exiting from the sixth oval bead from the beginning of the necklace.

5 String: 3 mm gold bead, 7 mm wooden bead, bead tube, 7 mm wooden bead, 3 mm gold bead, animal bead, 2.5 mm gold bead. Skipping the last bead, return through the animal bead and all the beads to the top wooden bead. String a 3 mm gold bead. Pass through the next oval bead on the necklace. Pull the bead tube fringe assembly snug, but not too tight, as you want it to swing freely below the round bead between each oval bead. Make a half-hitch knot around the necklace bead wire.

6 Repeat step 5 for the remaining 11 bead tubes.

7 When all the bead tubes are strung, pass through a few wooden beads on the necklace and make a half-hitch knot around the necklace bead wire. Repeat two or three more times to the end of the necklace.

8 Put the S-hook clasp on one of the split rings.

TIP Some dyed bead colors may fade with exposure to sunlight. A slight fading can be attractive in this project.

You'll need:

necklace, approximately 18 in. (46 cm) with 2½ in. (6.4 cm) pendant beads
- 11º cylinder beads, 5 g each:
  - squash
  - sienna
  - terracotta
  - pumpkin
  - brown
  - red
  - green
- 12 gold African animal beads
- 23 8 x 10 mm oval brown wooden beads
- 54 7 mm round brown wooden beads
- 12 2.5 mm round gold beads
- 38 3 mm round gold beads
- beading wire, preferably black or dark brown, .019
- Fireline, 8-lb–10-lb. test, smoke
- beading needle
- 2 gold crimp beads
- 2 6 mm gold split rings
- S-hook clasp

bangle, approximately 3 in. (7.6 cm) diameter
- 11º cylinder beads, 5 g each:
  - squash
  - sienna
  - terracotta
  - pumpkin
  - brown
  - red
  - green
- 30 black crow beads
- 1 yd. (.9 m) 1 mm leather cord

earrings
- 11º cylinder beads, 1 g each:
  - squash
  - sienna
  - terracotta
  - pumpkin
  - brown
  - red
- 4 7 mm round brown wooden beads
- 2 3 mm round gold beads
- 2 domed gold post earrings with loop
- 2 gold head pins

all projects
- white beading thread
- straws
- needle
- scissors
- chainnose or crimping pliers
- wire cutters

bangle

TIP Earthy African colors spiced with red and green make stunning beads to string on leather cord. Wear one, two, three, or more bracelets at a time. Have fun using colors in your favorite combinations!

1 Working in flat peyote, make the beads of your choice using the charts. You'll need 6–8 beads for each bracelet. Use the different lengths of the beads to help you make bracelets the same length, but vary the beads on each one. Fill each bead with a straw.

2 Cut a 12-in. (30 cm) piece of leather cord. String one crow bead and one bead tube, repeating until all the bead tubes for the bracelet are added, ending with a crow bead.

3 Tie the ends of the bracelet together with a square knot, making sure that it will still slip over your hand without untying it. Trim the ends of the leather cord to an inch or less, and tie an overhand knot close to the each end of the cord.

TIP Use permanent markers to color the white thread on the ends of the beads, if you wish.

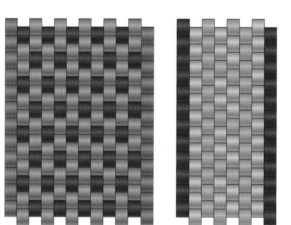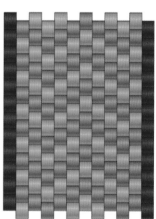

The bracelets are simple bangles on leather cord; the earrings are two favorite patterns and color combinations.

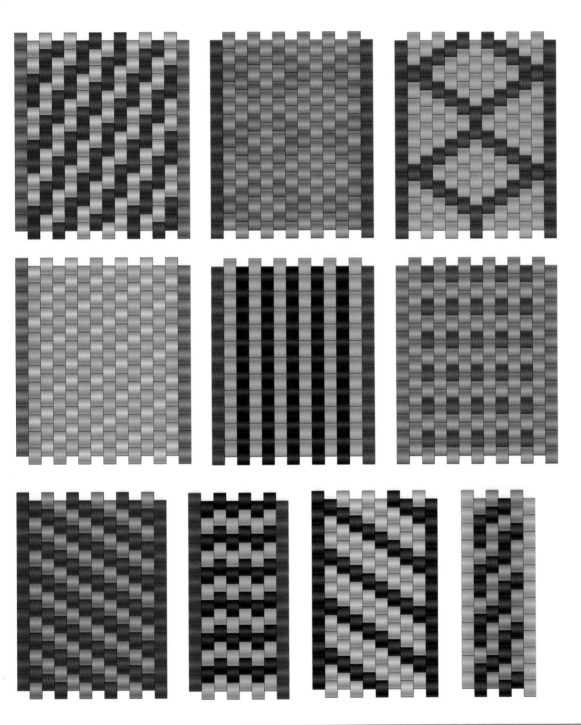

earrings

1 Following the charts and working in flat peyote stitch, make one bead tube from each chart. Fill each bead with a straw.

2 On a head pin, string a 3 mm round gold bead, a 7 mm round wooden bead, a bead tube, and a 7 mm round wooden bead. Make a loop. Attach to an earring finding.

3 Make a second earring.

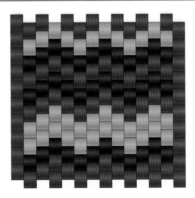
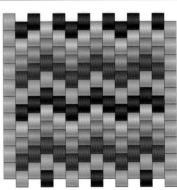

Delft Bracelet

For a traditional look, nothing beats cobat blue and white in a delicate design. Inspired by familiar Dutch delft patterns that were copied from early Chinese designs, I created these beads using simple geometric charts. The chunky cobalt blue accent beads with their white linings mirror the colors of the patterned beads.

Delft 1

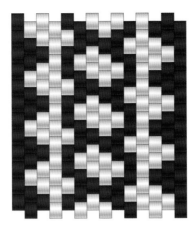

Delft 2

Delft 3

You'll need:

bracelet, 7½ in. (19.1 cm)

- 11º cylinder beads
  - 5 g white
  - 5 g cobalt blue
- 6 10 mm cobalt whiteheart beads
- 12 10 mm gold saucer spacer beads
- 2 3 mm gold cube beads
- 2 gold crimp beads
- gold clasp
- gold beading wire, .019
- white beading thread
- straws or filler beads
- needle
- scissors
- chainnose or crimping pliers
- wire cutters

1 Working in flat peyote stitch, make two beads each using the Delft 1 and Delft 2 charts. Make one bead using the Delft 3 chart. Insert straws into each bead or, if using filler beads, insert during the bracelet assembly.

2 Cut a 11-in. (28 cm) length of beading wire.

String a cube bead → saucer bead → cobalt bead → saucer bead

Delft 1 bead tube → saucer bead → cobalt bead → saucer bead

Delft 3 bead tube → saucer bead → cobalt bead → saucer bead

Delft 2 bead tube → saucer bead → cobalt bead → saucer bead

Delft 1 bead tube → saucer bead → cobalt bead → saucer bead

Delft 2 bead tube → saucer bead → cobalt bead → saucer bead

cube bead.

3 String a crimp bead and half of the clasp, and go back through the crimp bead. Crimp. Repeat on the other end of the bracelet with the other half of the clasp. Trim any excess wire.

Heart Cluster Necklace

Valentine's Day seems to call for some romantic hearts-and-flowers jewelry, although this necklace works as well for other occasions. A set of heart charms, some bead tubes in red, white, and gold, and a lock-and-key toggle clasp create a clustered pendant. Too bad I couldn't sneak on a few chocolates as well!

1 Make seven to ten bead tubes, substituting your choice of red, white, and gold beads and following charts from the Delhi Delight bracelet (p. 30), Chinese Coin Charm Earrings (p. 36), Geographical Bracelet (p. 66), or Bead Tube Soup Bracelet (p. 88).

TIP This is a good way to use up small amounts of beads from other projects.

2 On a head pin, string a gold seed bead, a larger gold bead, a bead tube, and a large gold bead. Make a loop. Repeat for each bead tube.

3 Decide on the order of the bead tubes and charms for the pendant. Placing large or especially ornate charms at the bottom of the chain works well.

4 Attach each charm and bead tube to the chain, one or two in each link, using jump rings. Cluster the charms and bead tubes on the last 3 in. (7.6 cm) of the chain.

5 After all the charms and tubes are added, attach the loop half of the toggle clasp to the chain in a link just above the last charm or bead tube.

6 Attach the other half of the toggle clasp to the other end of the chain.

7 The necklace will fasten in the front, allowing the beads and charms to fall in a cluster. You might need to move some of the charms and tubes around on the chain so they drape in a pleasing arrangement.

You'll need:

necklace, 22 in. (56 cm)
- 7–10 g 11° cylinder beads in your choice of colors:
  - white
  - silver-lined gold
  - light Siam
  - Siam
  - silver-lined red
  - red
  - dark red
- 10–12 heart charms
- 14–20 10–15 mm gold beads of various types
- lock-and-key toggle clasp
- 22 in. gold chain
- 7–10 3-in. (7.6 cm) gold head pins
- 24–32 4–8 mm gold jump rings
- white beading thread
- straws
- needle
- scissors
- chainnose pliers
- roundnose pliers
- wire cutters

Geographical Bracelet

Combine geometric and graphic patterns in contrasting black and white for a fascinating bracelet. If you use gold or a dark color like cranberry for the trim instead of primary colors, you'll create an entirely different look.

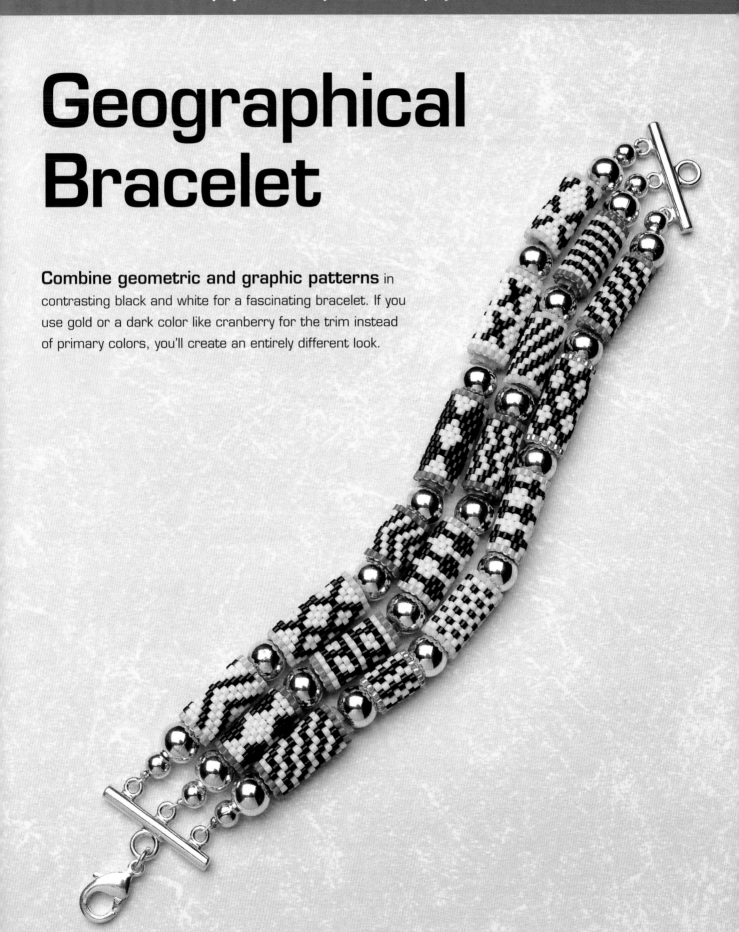

TIP The bracelet is made of short tubes of even- and odd-count peyote stitch. Each bead tube has a geometric pattern in black and white, trimmed with a row of color on each end. You'll need six to eight bead tubes for each bracelet strand. There are 24 different geometric patterns, some quite short, some long. By reversing the black and white in each graph, you can double the number. The reversed colors often make a very different-looking bead tube. Vary the bead tubes on each strand, and use the various lengths of the bead tubes to make the three strands the same length.

1 Working in flat peyote stitch, follow the charts to make bead tubes of your choice. Insert a straw in each bead tube.

2 Cut three pieces of beading wire about 12 in. (30 cm) long.

3 String a crimp bead on the beading wire. Pass the end of the beading wire through one of the loops on the bar clasp and back through the crimp bead. Pull snug. Crimp. Repeat with the other two strands of beading wire.

4 On one of the beading wires, string a 5 mm silver bead and an 8 mm silver bead. String a bead tube and an 8 mm silver bead six times. At the end of the strand, add a 5 mm silver bead and a crimp bead. Pass through a loop on the other bar clasp, and go back through the crimp bead and a few more beads. Pull snug. Crimp. Trim excess wire. Repeat for the two remaining strands.

TIP For a finishing touch, color the white thread showing at each end of the bead tube with a permanent ink marker to match the trim beads.

You'll need:

bracelet, 8 in. (20 cm), including clasp
- 11º cylinder beads
    - 12 g glossy black
    - 12 g white
    - 1 g light Siam
    - 1 g chartreuse
    - 1 g green
    - 1 g orange
    - 1 g matte yellow
    - 1 g lilac
    - 1 g opaque light blue
- 21 8 mm round silver beads
- 6 5 mm round silver beads
- 6 crimp beads
- silver bar clasp with three loops
- beading wire, .019
- white beading thread
- straws
- needle
- scissors
- chainnose or crimping pliers
- wire cutters
- permanent markers to match trim beads (optional)

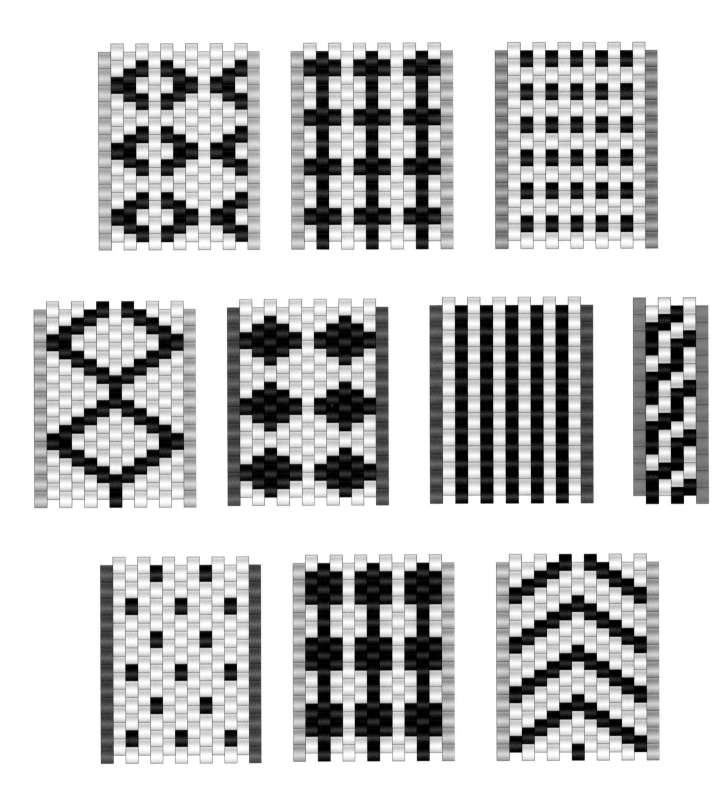

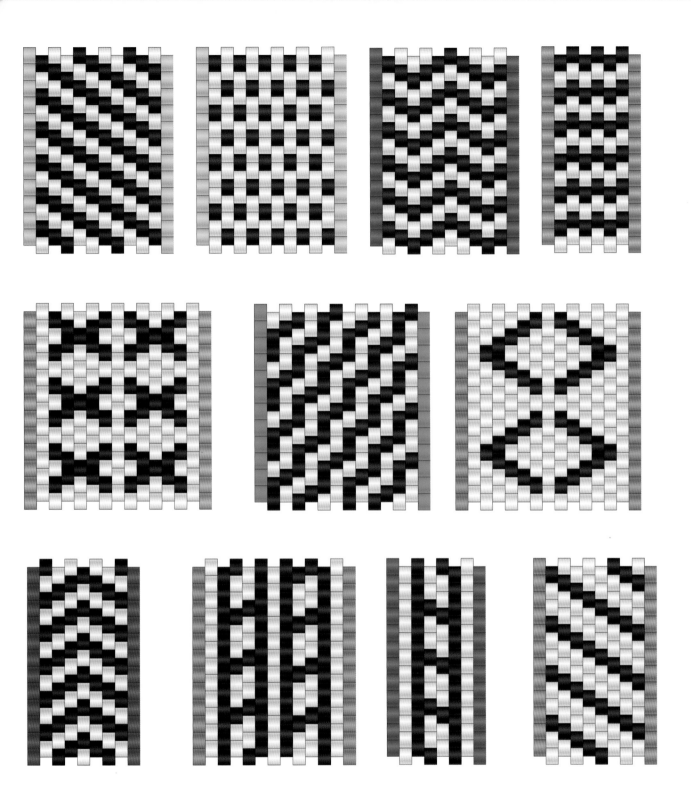

TIP The Safari Bracelet uses some of the same patterns, but in completely different colors. Did you realize that they were the same? Take a closer look.

Rainbow Bangle Bracelet

Here's something special for all of us who love rainbows. Use two bangle bracelets with loops; make beads to fit between and hope for summer showers, knowing your rainbow will always go with you. Add some bells (and whistles), if you like.

TIP Use permanent markers to color white beading thread to match the bead colors. Thread color showing through transparent beads will affect the overall color of the beadwork. It's amazing how white, light blue, and dark blue threads will make a difference in the way a transparent blue bead appears. Experiment with a few rows of each color to see the difference yourself.

1 For the inner core, make a ladder four seed beads long. Join the ends to make a circle. Work in tubular brick stitch for five more rows.

2 For the outer layer, string six seed beads. Work in flat peyote for a total of 20 rows (10 beads on each side). Wrap the peyote strip around the bead tube from step 1. Zip the ends together.

3 Repeat steps 1 and 2, making two bead tubes of each color.

4 On a eye pin, string a 5 mm round metal bead. Insert the tip of the eye pin through a loop on the bangle bracelet from the outside. String one of the completed bead tubes, passing the eye pin through the center of the core bead tube, and exit through a loop on the other bangle bracelet. String a 5 mm round metal bead. Make a loop similar in size to the eye pin loop on the other end.

5 Repeat step 4 for all 16 beads. The rainbow color order is repeated twice on the bracelet, with the crystal bead tubes separating the two rainbows.

6 Optional: Attach bells or other charms on jump rings and attach the jump rings to the eye pin loops.

TIP Remember, the rainbow is ROYGBIV: red, orange, yellow, green, blue, indigo (blue-violet), and violet.

You'll need:

- 11º seed beads, 2 g each:
  - transparent red
  - transparent orange
  - transparent yellow
  - transparent green
  - transparent blue
  - transparent indigo (blue-violet)
  - transparent violet
  - transparent crystal or clear
- 2 bangle bracelets with 16 loops on each
- 32 5 mm round metal beads
- 16 eye pins
- 32 bells or other charms or crystals (optional)
- 32 4 mm jump rings (optional)
- beading thread to match bead colors
- needle
- scissors
- chainnose pliers
- roundnose pliers
- wire cutters
- permanent markers (optional)

Dotted Ribbon Necklace

This quick and easy necklace is made of just three dotted bead tubes on a dotted ribbon necklace. Simply choose your favorite two or three colors to play with. Other charts in this book would make a colorful contrast to a different ribbon, such as stripes or a plaid—try a few different combinations for effortless style.

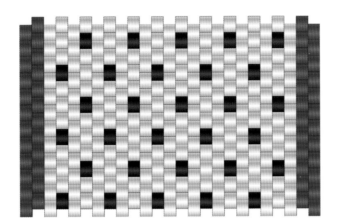

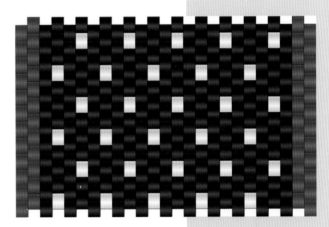

You'll need:

necklace, 16 in. (41 cm) plus clasp

- 11º cylinder beads
    - 3 g white
    - 2 g glossy black
    - 1 g red
- white and black beading thread
- dotted ribbon with clasp
- needle
- scissors

1 Working in flat peyote stitch, follow the charts, make three bead tubes.

TIP Notice that the borders on the beads in the photograph are two-drop brick (see Stitch How-tos). You can use regular one-drop brick stitch or flat peyote stitch to make the beads, but I like the stacked borders. The charts show the flat peyote version.

2 Slide beads onto the ribbon. How easy does it get? Have fun!

TIP I bought the ribbon with the clasp attached, but you can easily make one with a piece of ribbon, two cord tips, and a clasp. Connect a clasp and a chain on each end of the cord tip with jump rings.

Blue, Blue Sky Earrings

Haven't you always wanted everything? Here it is—the stars, the moon, and the blue, blue sky. Turquoise-colored jewelry is beautiful with either silver or gold. Experiment to find your personal favorite.

1 String two silver-lined gold beads, 18 turquoise beads, and two silver-lined gold beads. Work in flat peyote stitch for a total of 14 rows (seven beads on each side). Zip the ends together. Make two bead tubes.

2 String a silver-lined gold bead, 14 turquoise beads, and a silver-lined gold bead. Work in flat peyote stitch for 14 rows (seven beads on each side). Zip the ends together. Make four bead tubes.

3 Glue a small bead tube to each side of a large bead tube, centering the small tubes on each side of the large tube. Repeat for the other earring. Let dry thoroughly.

4 Attach a charm to each of the eye pin loops using a jump ring.

5 On the eye pin, string one of the assembled bead units from step 3, passing through the center of the large bead tube. Make a plain loop. Attach to the loop of the earring post with a jump ring.

6 Repeat steps 4 and 5 to make a second earring.

You'll need:

earrings
- 15º seed beads
  - 4 g turquoise
  - 1 g silver-lined gold
- star charm
- moon charm
- pair of gold ear wires
- 2 gold eye pins
- 4 small gold jump rings
- gold beading thread
- E6000 adhesive
- needle
- scissors
- chainnose pliers
- roundnose pliers
- wire cutters

Dragon's Treasure Set

This rich and mystical jewelry set is made from sparkling metallic cylinder beads filled and banded with golden treasure. Finish with a hidden clasp to keep the dragon's hoard safe and secure.

TIP The bracelet has 21 tube beads composed of a two-drop brick stitch border on each end and 20 rows of color and pattern between. The beads are linked by bands of ladder stitch. The clasps are hidden in the two end beads. Many people can slide the bracelet on like a bangle rather than using the clasps, as the bracelet has a certain amount of "stretch."

bracelet

1 Start each bead tube by making a two-drop ladder 12 beads long with the silver-lined gold beads. Join the ends to make a circle.

TIP Stitching a two-drop ladder means to make each stitch with two beads, one on top of the other, instead of using one bead for each stitch. Start a two-drop ladder with four beads, making two stacks of two beads each. Then continue making each stitch with two beads stacked one on top of the other. See the Stitch How-tos for extra help, if needed.

2 Working in tubular brick stitch (one bead per stitch), stitch a 20-row bead tube (see Bead Patterns chart).

3 At the end row of main color beads (row 22 overall), stitch one row of two-drop brick stitch in silver-lined gold beads.

This will match the two-drop ladder that starts the bead.

Bead patterns

Make seven plain tube beads, one of each main color.

Make seven tube beads with a pattern of rings, using a different main color for each tube bead and silver-lined gold beads for the rings. Make the rings at these beads:

1 ring at row 6 (counting just the main-color rows)
2 rings (rows 8 and 11)
2 rings (rows 7 and 14)
3 rings (rows 7, 11, and 14)
4 rings (rows 6, 10, 13, and 15)
5 rings (rows 2, 6, 10, 14, and 18)
5 rings (rows 4, 6, 8, 11, and 17)

Make seven tube beads with a spiral pattern, using a different main color for each tube bead and silver-lined gold beads for the spirals. Begin the spirals at these beads:

1 spiral beginning at bead 1
2 spirals beginning at beads 1 and 3
2 spirals beginning at beads 1 and 4
2 spirals beginning at beads 1 and 8
3 spirals beginning at beads 1, 3, and 6
3 spirals beginning at beads 1, 4, and 7
3 spirals beginning at beads 1, 5, and 9

TIP You can make one bead tube slightly larger (14 beads instead of 12) for the bead that will hold the clasp, which will make steps 7 and 8 easier.

You'll need:

bracelet, approximately 7½ in. (19.1 cm)
- 11º cylinder beads, 7 g in each main color
  - steel
  - dark metallic steel
  - metallic bronze
  - light metallic bronze
  - plated palladium
  - silver-lined bronze
  - silver-lined light bronze
- 20 g cylinder beads, silver-lined gold
- 2 gold bayonet-style magnetic clasps, 4 x 9 mm

necklace, approximately 18 in. (46 cm)
- 11º cylinder beads
  - 20 g steel
  - 3 g dark metallic steel
  - 3 g metallic bronze
  - 4 g light metallic bronze
  - 3 g plated palladium
  - 5 g silver-lined bronze
  - 4 g silver-lined light bronze
  - 10 g silver-lined gold
- dragon charm, pewter
- S-clasp with split rings
- Fireline, 6-lb. test, smoke
- rattail cord, approximately 24 in. (61 cm)
- E6000 adhesive

earrings
- 11º cylinder beads
  - 2 g steel
  - 1 g silver-lined gold
- 2 dark silver or pewter 8º seed beads
- 2 pewter dragon charms
- pewter post earrings
- 2 pewter or dark silver eye pins

all projects
- gold beading thread
- straws (optional)
- needle
- scissors
- chainnose pliers
- roundnose pliers
- wire cutters

4 Make a total of 21 beads. Fill each bead tube with a straw.

5 Arrange the bead tubes in the order you wish to string them.

6 For the linking bands, make a two-drop ladder 46 beads long with silver-lined gold beads. The linking band should be just long enough to go through two bead tubes. Insert the band through a bead tube, and return through another bead tube to link them together. Sew the ends together firmly. Continue making linking bands and attaching the bead tubes together. Stop before adding the last bead tube. You can make the linking bands a little longer for a slightly larger bracelet, or a little smaller, as long as you can still connect the ends.

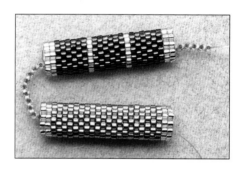

7 Make a two-drop ladder six beads long with silver-lined gold beads. Attach the cup portion of the clasp on each end of the band. This band should be just long enough to go through the bead tube and hide the clasp cups inside the bead tube. Insert into the last bead tube. This bead should not have a straw filler.

8 Make a two-drop ladder 46 beads long with silver-lined gold beads to attach the bead tube from step 7 to the end of the bracelet. Pull the band through the end bead tube and the clasp bead tube. This will be quite difficult; you may need a pair of long, sharp tweezers or pliers to work the linking band past the clasp cups.

9 Make a two-drop ladder 28 beads long with silver-lined gold beads. Attach the insertion end of the clasps on each end of

the band. This band should be just long enough to go through the first bead tube on the bracelet and insert into each of the cups concealed in the last bead tube made in steps 7 and 8.

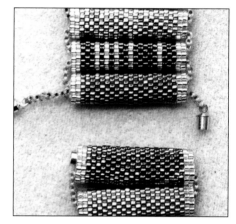

necklace

1 Using the Fireline, string 10 steel beads and one silver-lined gold bead. Tie into a circle, leaving an 8-in. (20 cm) tail.

2 Pass through the first bead strung. Start odd-count tubular peyote by stringing the color bead your thread is exiting, skipping a bead and going through a bead. Continue around the circle. Continue stringing the color bead you are exiting. Make the tube 18 in. (46 cm) long. After the first inch or two, work around the rattail cord.

3 At the end, secure the rattail cord inside each end of the tube with a few stitches through the rattail cord and the bead tube. Trim excess rattail cord.

4 Finish the end of the tube by decreasing every other steel bead until only two are left: To decrease, sew through the next up-bead without adding a bead. Leave the remaining Fireline to to attach the clasp later.

5 At the other end, thread the tail on a needle and repeat step 4.

Pendant

6 Start each tube bead by making a two-drop ladder 12 beads long with silver-lined gold beads. Join the ends to make a circle.

7 Work tubular brick stitch (one bead per stitch) using the main-color beads shown for the number of rows listed (see table below).

8 At the end of the main-color section of the tube bead, work one row of two-drop brick stitch in silver-lined gold beads. This will match the two-drop ladder that starts the tube bead.

9 For the top pendant tube bead, make a two-drop ladder of silver-lined gold beads 16 beads long. This tube bead will slide onto the tubular necklace, so be sure it fits around the necklace tube before joining the ends. Join the ends. Work in tubular brick stitch for 14 rows using steel beads. Finish with a two-drop brick stitch row of silver-lined gold beads.

10 Insert straws into each of the pendant tube beads. Glue the pendant tube beads together using E6000 adhesive, centering each tube bead over the previous tube bead in the order listed in the table.

TIP You may want to glue only a few pendant tube beads together at one time, letting each partial assembly dry throughly before adding another tube bead. Work on wax paper so the pendant does not stick to the working surface.

Pendant beads
Pendant beads, main-color rows, from bottom to top:
steel, 14 rows
bronze, 34 rows
silver-lined bronze, 44 rows
bronze, 54 rows
light bronze, 44 rows
palladium, 34 rows
dark steel, 24 rows

Finishing

11 Using E6000, glue the dragon charm to the assembled pendant. If the charm has a hanging loop, you may want to remove it first. Let dry throughly.

12 Slide the top tube bead of the pendant onto the necklace tube.

13 Using the remaining Fireline at each end of the necklace tube, attach the split rings for the S-clasp by sewing through the beads in the rings several times. Add the S-clasp.

earrings

1 Make a two-drop ladder 12 beads long with silver-lined gold beads. Join the ends to make a circle.

2 Work in tubular brick stitch (one bead per stitch) using the steel beads for four rows.

3 For row 7, skip the third and ninth beads, leaving a gap between the beads. The thread will stretch across the top of the gap. Do not pull the thread tight, which would cause the gap to close.

4 In row 8, when you come to the "missing" beads, bridge the gap by stringing a bead, looping under the thread that crosses the gap and passing back up through the bead as you would for a normal brick stitch. This adds the new bead and creates a small rectangular hole in the beadwork. At the end of the row, there will be two small holes on opposite sides of the tube bead in row 7.

5 Continue working in tubular brick stitch with steel beads for three rows.

6 Finish with a row of two-drop brick stitch in silver-lined gold beads.

7 Open the eye on the eye pin and attach it to the earring loop. String an 8° seed bead and a tube bead on the eye pin, passing through both holes in the beadwork. If you inserted a straw in the tube, you will probably need to pierce it with a needle before stringing the tube bead on the eye pin. Use the remaining portion of the eye pin to pass through the loop on the dragon charm. Make a loop.

8 Make a second earring.

Sea Dragon Bracelet

If the fiery dragon has his metallic treasure bracelet, doesn't a sea dragon deserve a bracelet in her sea-blue and sea-green colors with frothy silver-lace foam? Wear this ocean-inspired jewel with the Beach Glass Necklace and Earrings.

TIP Metallic-finish and silver-lined beads can sometimes tarnish, or the color may rub off. Dyed beads may also experience some fading. If you aren't sure how permanent a finish may be, add this step to protect your bead tubes before assembling your project: Dip the bead tubes in a small bowl of clear acrylic floor finish, drain the beads, and dry them on wax paper.

1 Follow steps 1–9 from the Dragon's Treasure Set bracelet, p. 76. Substitute aquas, mint green, teal, and opal beads for the main colors, and use silver-lined crystal beads instead of silver-lined gold beads for the rings and spirals.

TIP You can create a bracelet like this using any of the patterns in this book. Try a wild and colorful version with the Safari Set or Geographical Bracelet. Use primary colors or a dark palette for a truly showstopping piece!

You'll need:

bracelet, approximately 7½ in. (19.1 cm)
- 11º cylinder beads, 7 g each:
  - aqua blue
  - pale aqua
  - green aqua
  - light aqua
  - mint green
  - teal
  - sea opal
- 20 g 11º cylinder beads, silver-lined crystal
- 2 4 x 9 mm magnetic bayonet-style clasps, silver
- white beading thread
- straws
- needle
- scissors

Thai Memories

Aqua, white, and orange remind me of Thailand, where the food is good, the colors are fabulous, and the people are friendly. It is especially exciting to take an elephant ride through the jungle, swaying back and forth. Imagine your own exotic vacation while creating this colorful jewelry set.

bracelet

1 Working in flat peyote, follow the chart to make 10 bead tubes. If you need a longer bracelet, make additional pairs of bead tubes. (Be sure to increase the number of orange jade beads and spacers, too.)

2 Cut a 12-in. (30 cm) piece of beading wire, and string a crimp bead and one of the loops of the clasp. Pass back through the crimp bead and crimp. Repeat for the other bracelet strand.

3 On one of the bracelet beading wires, string an 8º silver seed bead.

4 String an orange jade bead, a silver spacer, a bead tube, and a silver spacer. Repeat four times.

5 Finish with an orange jade bead, an 8º silver seed bead, and a crimp bead. Pass the beading wire through a loop on the clasp and back through the crimp bead and a few other beads. Crimp. Trim the excess beading wire.

6 Repeat steps 3–5 for the other bracelet strand.

You'll need:

bracelet, approximately 7 in. (18 cm)
- 11º cylinder beads
  - 8 g aqua
  - 8 g white
  - 1 g orange
- 4 8º matte silver seed beads
- 12 6 mm round orange jade beads
- 20 6 x 1 mm silver spacers
- 4 crimp beads
- silver clasp with two loops
- beading wire, .019

earrings
- 11º cylinder beads
  - 2 g aqua
  - 2 g white
  - 1 g orange
- 4 8º matte silver seed beads
- 4 6 mm round orange jade beads
- 4 6 x 1 mm silver spacers
- 2 3-in. (7.6 cm) silver head pins
- pair of silver ear wires

necklace, 24 in. (61 cm) plus 2-in. (5 cm) pendant
- 11º cylinder beads
  - 3 g aqua
  - 3 g white
  - 1 g orange
- 24 in. silver necklace
- 6 8º matte silver seed beads
- 6 6 mm round orange jade beads
- 6 6 x 1 mm silver spacers
- 3 3-in. silver head pins
- 3 silver split rings

all projects
- white beading thread
- straws or filler beads
- needle
- scissors
- chainnose pliers
- roundnose pliers
- wire cutters

earrings

1 Working in flat peyote stitch, follow the chart to make two bead tubes.

2 On a head pin, string: 8º silver seed bead, orange jade bead, silver spacer, earring bead tube, silver spacer, orange jade bead, 8º silver seed bead.

3 Make a plain loop, and attach to an ear wire.

4 Make a second earring.

Earring bead

necklace

1 Working in flat peyote stitch, follow the charts to make one bead from the earring chart and one from each of the two necklace charts.

2 On a head pin, string: 8º silver seed bead, orange jade bead, silver spacer, necklace bead tube, silver spacer, orange jade bead, 8º silver seed bead.

3 Make a loop. Attach a split ring to the loop.

4 Repeat for the other two necklace bead tubes.

5 String the three necklace bead tubes on the necklace chain.

Necklace bead 1

Necklace bead 2

Beach Glass

At the beach, I always find pieces of sea-worn glass and wonder where they came from and how they ended up there. I wanted to make something to remind me of mellow days on the sand, watching the surf roll in, looking for shells and driftwood. To personalize your version, add charms or glass in different shades.

TIP Blue cylinder beads in transparent, opal, silver-lined, AB, and pearl finishes are best for this necklace. You can make every bead different using leftover beads from other projects, or buy special colors to complement your beach glass.

necklace

1 Stitch a two-drop ladder 12 beads long with the silver-lined crystal beads. Join the ends to make a circle.

TIP To create a two-drop ladder, see Stitch How-tos.

2 Work in tubular brick stitch (one bead per stitch) in your choice of blue for 20 rows.

3 Finish the bead tube with a row of two-drop brick stitch using silver-lined crystal beads.

4 Make eight beads total.

TIP You can also make the bead tubes for this project in flat peyote stitch. If you want a stacked border look, use two-drop peyote stitch on the edges; otherwise, work one-drop peyote stitch. To start the flat peyote version, string two silver-lined crystal beads, 20 blue beads, and two silver-lined crystal beads. Continue by working the silver-lined crystal beads as one-drop or two-drop and the blue beads in regular one-drop peyote. Work 24 rows (12 beads on each side). Zip the ends together.

5 Cut a 30-in (76 cm) length of beading wire. String: 8 mm round silver bead, bead tube, 8 mm round silver bead, beach glass bead, saucer bead, beach glass bead. Repeat six more times.

6 String: 8 mm round silver bead, bead tube, 8 mm round silver bead, two 5 mm round silver beads, two crimp beads. Go through half of the clasp and back through the crimp beads and silver beads. Crimp and trim the excess wire.

7 On the other end of the necklace, string two 5 mm round silver beads and two crimp beads. Go through the other half of the clasp and back through the crimp beads and silver beads. Crimp and trim the excess wire.

earrings

1 Stitch a two-drop ladder 12 beads long with silver-lined crystal beads. Join the ends.

2 Work in tubular brick stitch (one bead per stitch) in your choice of blue beads for eight rows.

3 Finish the bead tube with a row of two-drop brick stitch using silver-lined crystal beads.

TIP To work a flat peyote version, string two silver-lined crystal beads, eight blue beads and two silver-lined crystal beads. Continue by working the silver-lined crystal beads as one-drop or two-drop and the blue beads in regular one-drop peyote. Work 24 rows (12 beads on each side). Zip the ends together.

4 On an eye pin, string a 5 mm round silver bead, a bead tube, and a 5 mm round silver bead. Make a plain loop.

5 Attach the charms to the eye pin with jump or split rings.

6 Open the loop of an ear wire and attach the bead assembly.

7 Make a second earring.

You'll need:

necklace, approximately 24 in. (61 cm)
- 15 g 11º cylinder beads in several shades of blue
- 3 g 11º cylinder beads, silver-lined crystal
- 14 10 x 12 mm glass or resin beads in irregular shapes
- 16 8 mm round silver beads
- 4 5 mm round silver beads
- 7 20 x 8 mm silver saucer beads
- silver S-clasp with jump rings
- beading wire, .019
- 4 crimp beads

earrings
- 2 g 11º cylinder beads, blue
- 1 g silver-lined 11º cylinder beads
- 4 5 mm round silver beads
- 2 silver beach-theme charms
- pair of silver ear wires
- 2 silver eye pins
- 2 jump rings or split rings

both projects
- white beading thread
- needle
- scissors
- straws or filler beads
- chainnose pliers or crimping pliers
- roundnose pliers
- wire cutters

Bead Tube Soup Bracelet

Haven't you always wanted a big, floppy charm bracelet? Make one out of bead tubes! Feel free to add charms, lampworked beads, or found objects as well. Start with one bead on the bracelet, and add more as desired until you have a full, eye-catching piece.

TIP Use any of the charts in this book, or make up your own, to make bead tubes of various lengths. I've included 26 charts with this project to get you started. Remember that by reversing the colors in the chart, you'll get a completely different effect!

You'll need:

bracelet, approximately 7 in. (18 cm)

- 11º cylinder beads
  - 20 g opaque white
  - 20 g glossy black
  - small amounts in many colors
- silver charm bracelet or chain and clasp, approximately 7 in.
- 25–60 6 mm silver jump rings
- 25–60 silver head pins
- 50–120 6 mm silver round beads
- 5 g silver 11º seed beads
- white beading thread
- straws or filler beads
- needle
- scissors
- chainnose pliers
- roundnose pliers
- wire cutters

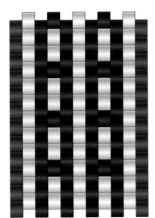

1 Make a bead tube using one of these charts or any of the other charts in the book.

2 Insert a straw (or filler beads) in the bead tube.

3 On a head pin, string a silver seed bead, a 6 mm round silver bead, the bead tube, and a 6 mm round silver bead. Make a plain loop.

4 Attach the assembled bead tube component to a link on the bracelet using a jump ring.

5 Repeat steps 1–4 to create as many beads as you'd like.

TIP This bracelet has 56 bead tubes, two or three per chain link. The shortest bead tubes on this bracelet have a pattern 12 beads wide, and the longest tubes are 25 beads wide. The geometric charts in the book use as few as 9 and as many as 27 beads. Use large- and small-diameter designs for even more variety.

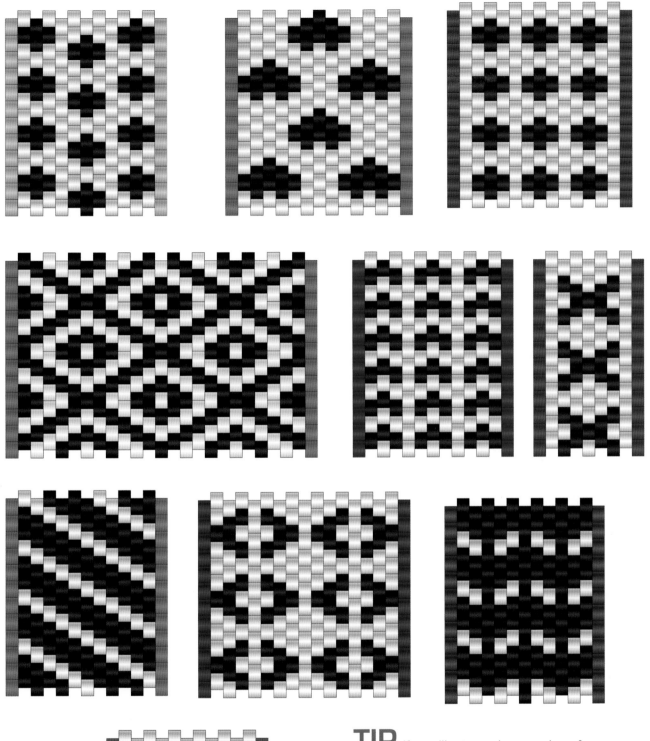

TIP If you like to make samples of your color choices before starting a project, you can save the beads to create a playful sampler bracelet of many colors.

Golden Columns

Simple, elegant, and quick, this necklace can be made in an hour and worn tonight. (The earrings will take another hour.) So much glamour for so little work! It does so much for a simple black T-shirt and slacks that I wear it frequently and always get compliments. It would look good with a low-cut neckline too.

necklace

1 Make a ladder 10 beads long. Join the ends.

2 Work in tubular brick stitch for another 30 rows.

3 On the next row (row 32), skip the third and eighth beads. You will have thread bridging the gaps. Do not pull the thread tight, which would cause the gaps to close.

4 On row 33, when you come to the "missing" beads, bridge the gap by stringing a bead, looping under the thread that crosses the gap, and passing back up through the bead as you would for normal brick stitch. This adds the new bead and creates a small rectangular hole in row 32. There should be two small holes on opposite sides of the bead tube.

5 Work two more rows and end the thread.

6 Pass the narrow bayonet-style clasp of the necklace through the two holes in the bead tube, suspending the tube from the necklace. (If you use some other type of necklace, pass the necklace wire through the holes and add the clasp afterward.)

earrings

1 Make a ladder four beads long. Join the ends.

2 Work in tubular brick stitch for another 11 rows.

3 On the next row (row 13), start the row with one bead instead of the normal two. Skip the second and fourth beads. You will have thread bridging the gaps. Do not pull the thread tight.

4 On row 14, when you come to the gap, bridge it by stringing a bead, stringing a bead, looping under the thread that crosses the gap, and passing back up through the bead as you would for normal brick stitch.

5 Work one more row and end the thread.

6 Slide the completed earring tube on the hoop.

7 Make a second earring.

TIP If the earring tube seems crooked, insert a head pin or wire cut to length to keep it straight.

You'll need:

necklace, 18 in. (46 cm) with a 2¼-in. (5.7 cm) pendant
- 5 g 11º gold-lined seed beads
- multistrand wire necklace with slender clasp

earrings
- 2 g 11º gold-lined seed beads
- ¾ in. (1.9 cm) hoop earrings, very slender

both projects
- gold beading thread
- needle
- scissors

Bead Guide

For the projects in this book, I used Delicas, a brand of cylinder bead manufactured by Miyuki. Here's a guide to the exact colors I used.

Bead Tube Soup Bracelet
DB200 White Opaque Delicas
DB10 Glossy Black Delicas

Beach Glass
Blue Delica beads in several shades
DB41 Silver-lined Crystal Delicas

Blue, Blue Sky Earrings
15-413 Turquoise Blue Opaque seed beads
15-003 Silver-lined Gold seed beads

Bronze Columns
Matte Bronze Iridescent triangle beads
Bronze Iridescent twisted hex beads

Calligraphy Necklace
DB505 Dark Gold Delicas
DB762 Dark Cream Matte (ivory) Delicas
DB35 Galvanized Silver Delicas

Chakra Bracelet
DB783 Matte Violet Delicas
DB787 Matte Dark Aqua Delicas
DB793 Matte Opaque Turquoise Delicas
DB656 Matte Dark Jade Delicas
DB751 Matte Opaque Yellow Delicas
DB752 Matte Opaque Orange Delicas
DB796 Matte Opaque Dark Red Delicas
DB310 Matte Black Delicas

Chinese Coin Charm Earrings
DB757 Matte Opaque Lt. Siam and DB727 Opaque Lt. Siam Delicas, mixed
DB31 Bright Gold 24kt. Plated Delicas

Christmas Charm Bracelet
Green Delicas in one, two or three shades,
DB200 Opaque White Delicas

Copper and Silver Bracelet
DB35 Galvanized Silver Delicas

DB40 Copper Bright Plated Delicas
DB10 Glossy Black Delicas

Delft Bracelet
DB200 Opaque White Delicas
DB726 Opaque Cobalt Blue Delicas

Delhi Delight Set
DB42 Silver-lined Gold Delicas
DB722 Opaque Orange Delicas
DB721 Opaque Yellow Delicas
DB658 Opaque Turquoise Delicas
DB727 Opaque Lt. Siam Delicas
DB661 Opaque Purple Delicas
DB724 Opaque Green Delicas
DB1371 Opaque Rose Pink

Dotted Ribbon Necklace
DB200 Opaque White Delicas
DB10 Glossy Black Delicas
DB723 Opaque Red Delicas

Dotted Swiss Bracelet
DB237 Mint Ceylon Delicas
DB249 Purple Ceylon Delicas
DB232 Pale Lemon Ceylon Delicas
DB240 Sapphire Ceylon Delicas
DB236 Rose Ceylon Delicas
DB201 Pearl Ceylon Delicas

Dragon's Treasure Set
DB22 Bronze Metallic Delicas
DB22L Bronze Light Metallic Delicas
DB26 Steel Dark Metallic Delicas
DB38 Palladium Plated Delicas
DB150 Bronze Silver-lined Delicas
DB181 Light Bronze Silver-lined Delicas
DB21 Steel Delicas
DB42 Silver-lined Gold Delicas

Heart Cluster Necklace
DB200 Opaque White Delicas
DB42 Silver-lined Gold Delicas
DB757 Matte Opaque Lt. Siam Delicas
DB727 Opaque St. Siam Delicas
DB723 Opaque Red Delicas
DB602 Silver-lined Red Delicas
DB774 Matte Transparent Red Delicas
DB753 Dark Red Delicas

Geographical Bracelet
DB10 Glossy Black Delicas
DB200 Chalk White Delicas
DB727 Light Siam Delicas
DB733 Opaque Chartreuse Delicas
DB655 Opaque Kelly Green Delicas
DB7222 Opaque Orange Delicas
DB751 Opaque Matte Yellow Delicas
DB249 Ceylon Lilac Delicas
DB215 Opaque Light Blue Delicas

Golden Columns Set
Gold-lined AB Crystal seed beads

Paramount Theater
DB661 Opaque Purple Delicas
DB1371 Opaque Rose Pink Delicas
DB 658 Opaque Turquoise Delicas
DB42 Gold-lined Crystal Delicas

Safari Set
DB651 Dyed Opaque Squash
DB794 Sienna Opaque Matte Dyed
DB389 Matte Opaque Lt. Terracotta
DB653 Dyed Opaque Pumpkin
DB734 Chocolate Brown
DB723 Opaque Red
DB656 Opaque Green

Sea Dragon
DB079 Lined Aqua Blue AB Delicas
DB083 Transparent Pale Aqua AB Delicas
DB238 Lined Crystal Green Aqua Luster Delicas
DB626 Light Aqua Green Silver-lined Alabaster Delicas
DB627 Mint Green Alabaster Delicas
DB1208 Silver-lined Caribbean Teal Delicas
DB1567 Opaque Sea Opal Luster Delicas
DB41 Silver-lined Crystal Delicas

Starry Night
DB10 Glossy Black and DB310 Matte Black Delicas, mixed
DB41 Silver-lined Crystal Delicas

Thai Memories
DB1595 Matte Opaque Sea Opal AB Delicas
DB200 Opaque White Delicas
TB174 Transparent Orange Toho Aikos

Tiny Venetians
15-1341 Medium Rose Silver-lined seed beads
15-519 Pink Ceylon seed beads
15-1202 Dark Cranberry Silver-lined seed beads

Topkapki Necklace
DB31 Bright Gold 24kt Plated Delicas
DB202 Pearl AB Delicas
DB216 Royal Blue Opaque AB Delicas
DB164 Light Blue Opaque AB Delicas

Voila! Earrings
Confetti earrings
DB200 Opaque White Delicas
DB42 Silver-lined Gold Delicas
DB602 Silver-lined Red Delicas
DB10 Glossy Black Delicas
DB1211 Silver-lined Gray Mist Delicas

Hannukah earrings
DB725M Opaque Light Blue Delicas
DB200 Opaque White Delicas
DB726 Opaque Cobalt Blue Delicas
DB42 Silver-lined Gold Delicas

Christmas earrings
DB45 Silver-lined Green Delicas
DB200 Opaque White Delicas
DB723 Opaque Red Delicas
DB42 Silver-lined Gold Delicas

Tibetan Fantasy
15-408 Dark Red Opaque seed beads
11-742 Turquoise Blue Opaque seed beads
11-590 Olive Grey Opal seed beads
15-413 Turquoise Blue Opaque seed beads
15-590 Olive Grey Opal seed beads

About the Author

Nancy Zellers is a bead engineer—a designer and a writer who truly enjoys creating amazing beadwork one little bead at a time. She takes seed beads and turns them into something different, bigger and totally unexpected using her analytical perspective and software design training.

Her first exposure to beadwork was in the '70s when she explored loomed beadwork and needlepoint. In the '90s, she took several art classes and started producing sculptural works with seed beads. These sculptures have appeared in over 28 local and national contemporary art exhibitions.

Nancy acquired new techniques and expanded her view of the bead world

through classes with many leading beadwork teachers. Branching out of the solitary artist's studio, she began designing jewelry pieces and developing instructional material. She has published more than 35 articles in magazines and books. She has been teaching on the local and national level for more than 10 years.

Nancy designs beadwork that is extremely wearable, and she loves strong colors and clean lines. She can usually be found in her hot-pink-and-lime-green studio in Denver, sewing one little bead to another little bead. Contact Nancy at www.nzbeads.com.

Acknowledgments

Over my years of beading, I've learned many things from many people; some in classes, some one-on-one, some via books and magazines, and some from the Internet. Some, but certainly not all, of the people I have learned useful beading stitches and techniques from include Carol Wilcox Wells, Carol Perrenoud and Virginia Blakelock (who were among my earliest teachers), David Chatt, Diane Fitzgerald, and Julia Pretl, as well as my wonderful students who teach me new things every year. They are all just amazing and fabulously generous about sharing knowledge.

No author can write a book without the help of friends. My two faithful and constant aides, much put-upon, are Carol Oakes and Linda McGill. Both are endowed with great patience and a highly critical eye.

Over the past few years, my husband, Steve Shapland, has somewhat unwillingly become a very competent beader who is pressed

into service occasionally for beading projects, diagram drawing, instruction proofing, bead toting and all the other miscellaneous chores that fall to the handiest person available. He has endured it with (mostly) good cheer and a few good laughs at my beading world. I don't know what I would do without him and his support.

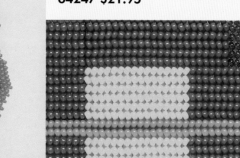

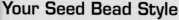
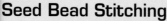
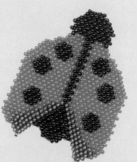